The Economy of Mauritania

Richard M. Westebbe

The Praeger Special Studies program—
utilizing the most modern and efficient book
production techniques and a selective
worldwide distribution network—makes
available to the academic, government, and
business communities significant, timely
research in U.S. and international economic, social, and political development.

The Economy of Mauritania

PRAEGER SPECIAL STUDIES IN INTERNATIONAL ECONOMICS AND DEVELOPMENT

Praeger Publishers   New York   Washington   London

PRAEGER PUBLISHERS
111 Fourth Avenue, New York, N.Y. 10003, U.S.A.
5, Cromwell Place, London S.W.7, England

Published in the United States of America in 1971
by Praeger Publishers, Inc.

Library of Congress Catalog Card Number: 74-151961

Printed in the United States of America

The Islamic Republic of Mauritania is culturally and ethnically one of emerging Africa's most fascinating case studies. Alfred Gerteiny, in his Mauritania (New York: Praeger, 1967), has written the definitive work in English on this aspect of the country. For those concerned with economic and social development, it is almost a classic case of the traditional economy and social structure confronted with the rapid growth of enclave-type islands of modern activity. The theme of this book, then, is the prospect and problems of development under conditions of economic dualism.

The book grew out of the unique experience of the author, who was charged by the World Bank, or International Bank for Reconstruction and Development (IBRD), with directing a mission to develop guidelines for a development strategy for the country. The success of this work and his subsequent involvement in advising the government at critical stages in its development planning and institution-building enable him to write authoritatively on this subject.

The government of Mauritania had, since independence, benefitted greatly from the aid and technical assistance involvement of France. It was not, however, satisfied that a coherent development strategy was being pursued and that the resources being devoted to development were having a suitable impact. Indeed, there was substantial evidence that, despite the vast investments made in the past, very little had changed for the average citizen of this new country. The author became deeply involved in that harsh but appealing country when he was appointed in 1967 as Chief of the IBRD's technical assistance mission, which spent three months in Mauritania at the request of the government in order to draw up guidelines for a new four-year development program.

It was the author's privilege and that of his colleagues on the mission to have the opportunity to make this fundamental reassessment for the Mauritanian Government. The mission started with an examination of the facts by economic sectors. What had been done, what was the result, and, most importantly, what could be done technically, economically, and socially. Everyone was aware that a population living in

v

relative harmony with its environment and employing the technology of prehistoric times could not be expected suddenly to adapt to the technology of the mid-twentieth century, even if this would have been economically desirable.

That the report and its recommendations were well received was not so much because of the mission's persuasiveness as advocates, the author would like to think, but, rather, because it presented a rational way of achieving the country's economic and social development objectives, consistent with human and financial resource constraints and with the traditions and culture of the basically rural Moorish-Negro population.

The author returned to Mauritania twice more to follow developments at the request of the government and to advise on particular problems and policies related to development planning. The progress being made in taking the mission's basic report and shaping it into a genuine Mauritanian instrument of development was impressive.

This book is, then, not only a description and analysis of a country's development problems and prospects, but much more a critical examination of Mauritania's development in the light of a new strategy of development, based on the rural sector, that requires a basic change in policies, resource allocation, and program preparation and implementation. The modern sector is dominated almost entirely by enclave-type iron- and copper-mining enterprises, developed with outside capital and skills that have virtually no important links with the traditional economy. The bulk of the population consists of nomadic livestock herders, who live on the sub-Saharan grasslands, and peasant farmers along the Senegal River.

The book examines the country's potential for development, with particular stress on the technical, economic, and social prospects for bringing about fundamental changes in the rural sector. In this connection, an examination is made of the nation's transportation, distribution, and marketing system, including the special problem of open borders with neighboring states. Special attention is paid to the workings of the former state organization to control the road-transport system and the existing state trading monopoly in basic foodstuffs. Education, public utilities, construction, and community development are considered in the light of Mauritania's development objectives and constraints.

The analysis starts with an assessment of the first four-year plan and its outcome. A review is made of its objectives, as well as the impact of investments made and policies pursued. Its weaknesses are appraised, including the serious problems of plan administration and the strategic errors in capital-intensive irrigation works, as well as the badly planned and executed fishing industry of the north. The new plan is then evaluated in terms of the experience of the past and the basic development potential and sectoral interdependencies identified in the analysis of the economic sectors.

The book devotes a good deal of attention to the constraint posed for development by the problems of acquiring and managing adequate resources. This causes the author to go deeply into the area of public finance and the public policy implications of the budget in relation to development planning requirements. In this connection, an examination is made of the tax burden, the Treasury, and the functioning of the monetary system. The critical role of foreign aid and investment is then related to the experience of the past and the requirements of the future in terms of likely availability of aid and Mauritania's absorptive capacity for aid and investment.

The final chapter reflects on the lessons of development derived from the Mauritanian experience, lessons that will have meaning for those concerned with bringing some of the least-developed nations of the world along the path to greater well-being for the bulk of their peoples and in terms that respond to the needs and desires of these people. These lessons concern the limitations of modern-sector growth and rapid urbanization for bringing about such development and the consequent necessity for building on the social structure and economic potential of the traditional activities in the early phases of development. Lessons are also drawn on what the author has termed the illusion of the benefits of foreign aid and related technology. The book ends with a call for real effort and involvement on the part of foreign aid agencies in hard-core projects for Mauritania's development.

Those involved in developing the country's economic resources know full well that there is no magic that will solve its development problems. Development will be a difficult and costly process. This book is an attempt to document this effort and its underlying strategy in a way that will be useful to others concerned with development. Accordingly, the author has not included exhaustive descriptions of all the known facts about every sector, which would have made this a longer, but less readable, work. Footnotes have been kept to the minimum needed to identify key sources. Part of the material for this book comes from internal official collections in France that contain reports and documents not available in the United States. A selected bibliography has been included for the scholar and more specialized reader.

ACKNOWLEDGMENTS

At the outset, I must acknowledge my debt to my colleagues and friends on the 1967 IBRD technical assistance mission. There is no way to weigh properly the benefit that I received from their enthusiastic cooperation and dedicated work, or even the long hours of discussion and debate while traveling through the interior or in the sparse rooms of the Marhaba Hotel in Nouakchott. I give particular thanks to Mustapha Zaanouni, who took a good deal of the responsibility for the agriculture and fisheries work, and to Livio Costa, who was responsible for the education work. Both of these men were there for most of the mission, as was Mustapha El Kouni, who acted as adviser and helped us interpret this complex culture. Henri Boumendil was responsible for hydrology, R. Aubrey for the basic work on fisheries, J. P. Marty for livestock, Gerard Lescannes for agronomy, and Pierre Chardon for mining.

Special thanks must go to my colleague from the IBRD, Albert Waterston, who came for two weeks to work with me on plan organization and whose insights were inspired. Finally, I must acknowledge the fine work done on transportation by Wilfred Thalwitz and his colleagues Bernard Siret and Lucien Brochet from the IBRD. Houng K. Thanh, adviser to the plan organization, was most helpful in facilitating my work, as well as serving as a valued colleague with whom I could discuss economic policy to great advantage.

The French Government and its embassy and aid mission in Nouakchott were particularly helpful and gave me valuable assistance during the period of my involvement in Mauritania. It would be difficult to mention all of the officials involved. In particular, I would like to thank Ambassador Costilhes and Cooperation Mission Director Aymard.

My work in Mauritania could not have been carried out without the full support and cooperation of His Excellency Moktar Ould Daddah, President of the Islamic Republic of Mauritania, members of his Cabinet, numerous public servants, and various members of the private sector. Two officials deserve particular mention because of the key roles that they played. They are Mokhtar Ould Haiba, Minister of Finance, and Mohamed Nassim Kochman, Mauritanian Executive Director at the IBRD and a dedicated, effective spokesman on its behalf.

Finally, I would like to acknowledge the patient, efficient work of my secretary, Miss Cristina Chuidian, who labored through the drafts of this book and kept the project on schedule.

Although I was a staff member of the IBRD while working in Mauritania, this book is a personal effort. I alone am responsible for the analysis and conclusions. The report, thus, may not be attributed to the IBRD and its affiliated organizations and may not be quoted as representing their views.

CONTENTS

LIST OF TABLES

Tables		Page

TABLES IN THE APPENDIX

Appendix Tables

LIST OF ABBREVIATIONS

AID	Agency for International Development
BCEAO	Banque Centrale des Etats de l'Afrique de l'Ouest
BIAO	Banque Internationale de l'Afrique Occidentale
BMD	Banque Mauritanienne de Développement
CFA	Communauté Financière Africaine
CFAF	Francs de la Communauté Financière Africaine
EEC	European Economic Community (Common Market)
EIB	European Investment Bank
FAC	Fonds d'Aide et de Coopération
FAO	Food and Agriculture Organization
FED	Fonds Europeens de Développement
IBRD	International Bank for Reconstruction and Development
IDA	International Development Association
IFC	International Finance Corporation
IMF	International Monetary Fund
MAURELEC	Société Mauritanienne d'Electricité
MICUMA	Société des Mines de Cuivre de Mauritanie

MIFERMA	Mines de Fer de Mauritanie
ONTP	Office National des Transports Publics
OPT	Office de Post et Télégraphe
RIM	République Islamique de Mauritanie
SAFELEC	Société Africaine d'Electricité
SCET	Société Centrale pour l'Equipement de Territoire
SEDES	Société d'Etuder Pour le Développement Economique et Sociale
SEM	Société d'Equipement de la Mauritanie
SMB	Société Mauritanienne de Banque
SMIG	Salaire minimum interprofessionel garanti
SOMAP	Société Mauritanienne d'Armement à la Pêche
SOMIMA	Société Minière de Mauritanie
SOMIP	Société Mauritanienne des Industries de la Pêche
SONIMEX	Société Nationale Import-Export
SUCIN	Société d'Urbanisme et de Construction Immobilière de Nouakchott
UMOA	Union Monétaire Ouest Africaine
UNDEAO	Union Douanière des Etats de l'Afrique de l'Ouest
UNDP	United Nations Development Program

PROFILE
OF
MAURITANIA

THE COUNTRY

AND

ITS PEOPLE

THE POLITICAL AND SOCIAL STRUCTURE

Mauritania achieved independence after sixty years of French rule in November, 1960.[1] The French did not fundamentally change the tribal and feudal structure that they found but, rather, modified it and gradually brought it under the control of government. Nevertheless, changes in the social structure were occurring that were hastened by a spreading European influence. These tended to reduce the rigid class distinctions of the Moorish tribal structure and the system of feudal tribute. The tribal structure of the Senegal River area had been subjected to European influence far earlier, as part of the process of European penetration along the river. The various Negro ethnic groups that inhabit the Senegal River basin were, consequently, exposed to larger and more profound French cultural and commercial influences.

The present Islamic Republic of Mauritania contains a population of which about 80 per cent are of Moorish background and about 20 per cent are of Negro origin. Although virtually all are Moslems, the former group has an Arab-Berber ethnic and cultural background, whereas the latter consists of such distinct Negro ethnic groups as Toucouleurs, Sarakoles, and Peuls.[2] The Moors trace their ancestry back to the Almoravides and their Hassaniya Arab successors, who had conquered Morocco and Spain, absorbed the Berber tribes, and spread Islam to the Negro tribes in Mauritania. The Negro tribes can also recall proud kingdoms that successively fought and

3

made treaties with the Moors and the French, a process that took place over centuries and that had as its focal point the Senegal River basin.

Mauritania has aptly been described as the bridge (trait d'union) between Arab Africa and Black Africa. Culturally and ethnically the majority of the population relates to the north, while the minority looks to the south. Materially, however, the country's main ties are with the south, particularly Dakar, with which the bulk of commerce takes place. Between Mauritania and the northern Arab states lies the barrier of the western Sahara desert, which effectively inhibits communication and large-scale trade.

The present political structure evolved, after independence, from a number of political parties that combined to create a single national party, the People's Party, and that, in effect, agreed to express their differences within this framework. Dissident elements in Morocco and at home were and are not considered a serious threat, in view of the general support that the party has had from the people. From the outset, the stress was on national unity. Governmental portfolios were distributed in order to effect a balance between the various interests involved. In 1961, a new constitution was voted, creating a Presidential system and vesting legislative power in a forty-member National Assembly. Moktar Ould Daddah was recognized as the dominant political leader and has, from the beginning, been head of the party, as well as President of the Republic.

Deputies to the National Assembly are elected on a national basis, with the various constituencies voting on candidates approved by the central party organization. Of the three Emirs surviving the French period, only one is alleged to retain real power over his domain. Yet the vast distances and isolated condition of the largely nomadic peoples tend to preserve a good deal of tribal control in the rural areas, a control that is only gradually being reduced, as evidenced by the emergence of new political figures who are not always members of the ruling families. An important and controversial step to advance the cause of modernization and to curb corruption was taken in 1964, when the party was made the principal instrument for formulating national policy and the power of the more traditionalist National Assembly was correspondingly reduced.

By far the most serious divisive factor exists between the dominant Moors and the minority Negro ethnic groups along the Senegal River. This is not entirely a matter of color,

since some 40 per cent of the Moors are the black descendants
of subject peoples who intermarried with the Moors and who
regard themselves as fully part of this group. The white
Moor, or bidan, constitutes the ruling class of Moorish society,
which does make color distinctions. The problem is also cultural, with the more militant Moorish groups desiring specifically to advance Arabic as the official language and the Negroes
demanding more influence and autonomy. The mother tongue
of the Negro groups is any of a number of tribal dialects.
These people, who usually also speak Arabic, were particularly
successful in adapting themselves in the past to the French
language and administration. As a result, they now hold a disproportionate number of places in the civil service, where
French is the official language, a position they are reluctant
to lose.

The issue erupted into serious disturbances in February,
1966, in the capital, mainly among students representing the
two groups, over the proposal of the Minister of Education to
enforce Arabic as the language of instruction in the secondary
schools. This led to the closing of the secondary schools in
Nouakchott and Rosso for the balance of the year. A subsequent Party Congress was followed by a thorough reorganization of the government and the decision not to change the
status quo. The reorganization placed special emphasis on
the youth, and a new High Commission was established for
this purpose. It is evident that the President has managed to
reestablish the former consensus between the two groups, and
the near-term prospects for continued stability are good in the
opinion of experienced observers.

In the field of foreign relations, Mauritania has succeeded
in establishing cordial relationships with virtually all nations
and blocs. It is a member of a number of African blocs, including that of the Arab nations, and has had good political
and economic relations with the USSR, the Chinese People's
Republic (Communist China), and the United States. It joined
other African states in breaking diplomatic relations with the
United Kingdom over the issue of Rhodesia and broke relations
with the United States following the Middle East conflict in
spring, 1967. Relations with the United States and the United
Kingdom were later reestablished.

Mauritania has close ties with France, which were formal-
ized in 1961 in a series of economic, financial, and technical
agreements. France is by far the largest single contributor
of concessional aid and technical assistance to Mauritania.
France also exercises strong cultural influences on the country,

particularly through the educational system. A number of
Frenchmen still occupy important administrative and judicial
posts in the government, although they are gradually being
replaced as trained Mauritanians become available. Mauritania
is a member of the West African Monetary Union (UMDA),
The Customs Union of West African States (UNDEAO) and the
Organization of Senegal River States. It is also one of the
eighteen African States associated with the Common Market
(European Economic Community, EEC), from which it receives
considerable economic assistance. Nevertheless, it has pursued a policy of increasing economic independence.

The country's principal external problem was the issue
of Morocco's nonrecognition of Mauritania's independence,
although there has recently been a reconciliation. The conflicting claims of the two nations to the Spanish Sahara (Río
de Oro) remain as a potential source of trouble. Little pres-
sure is being exerted on the Spanish by the Mauritanians, no
doubt in recognition of the dangers that a change in the status
quo of the Spanish Sahara would involve. Indeed, Mauritania
has important economic agreements with Spain in the Port-
Etienne (Nouadhibou) fishing industries, in which considerable
Spanish investment is anticipated.

The nation's foreign relations reflect the high degree of
moderation and pragmatism characteristic of internal relations
among the Moors. The pressures for development and the
stresses of social change are less likely to take on an explosive
character under these circumstances. Rather, it would appear that the authorities in Mauritania will have the time, if
they choose to use it, to marshal their limited resources in
a systematic manner to enable growth to proceed in an orderly
fashion.

THE PEOPLE AND THEIR ENVIRONMENT

According to the most recent sample census, Mauritania
had a population in 1965 estimated at 1,040,000. [3] A newer,
complete census may well reveal important differences in the
size and characteristics of the population from the estimates
used here. The urban population is not known with any pre-
cision but is reported to be slightly in excess of 10 per cent
of the total and is spread over a number of relatively small
towns. Nouakchott, the capital, has an estimated population
of between 20,000 and 32,000; Port-Etienne, Fort-Gouraud,

and Kaedi have about 10,000 each; and Rosso has some 5,000.
Growth has been most rapid in the towns that are part of the
modern sector, particularly Nouakchott, Port-Etienne, and
Fort-Gouraud.

The estimated rate of population growth is 1.7 per cent
annually; it is 1.5 per cent among the Moors and 1.9 per cent
among the Negroes. The growth rate of the small urban population may be as high as 3 per cent annually. This implies a
doubling of population in forty years and a net increase of some
300,000 by 1980. Life expectancy at birth is forty years.
Because of the primitive and harsh conditions of life in the
country, the child mortality rate up to one year of age is extremely high. Both the survival and death rates can be expected to change significantly in the event of a great improvement in public health services. In 1965, the country had
twenty-eight doctors, of whom four were nationals; three
hospitals; fifteen medical centers; and fifty-one dispensaries.
There were some 160 trained nurses, plus auxiliary personnel,
staffing most of these facilities. Despite the progress made
in recent years, it is evident that the bulk of the population
has no access to modern medical care.

The distribution of population reflects primarily ecological
conditions. The main factor determining the location and concentration of the population is the availability of water. Close
to 80 per cent of the population lives south of the 17th parallel
in one-seventh of the country's land area. The concentration
of population ranges from less than 0.1 per sq. km. in the
north to 8 per sq. km. in Guidimaka in the far south.

The outer limit of regular pasture terrain is marked by
the 100-mm. annual rainfall line that passes through the oasis
of Atar in the north (21st parallel) and is close to the 17th
parallel in the southwest. South of this 100-mm. line, annual
rainfall increases to some 600-mm. along the river in the
south. In areas where rainfall exceeds the 200-mm. level,
dry farming is found in addition to cattle, and the pure nomad
is replaced by the seminomad and sedentary population. In
general, the Moors are nomadic, whereas the Negroes tend
to be sedentary, although the distinction is not sharp.

The main movement of population is toward the south
from the Saharan and sub-Saharan zones to the more plentifully
watered Sahelien areas. Increased sedentarization is observa-
ble in the form of new villages and increases in the sizes of
regional towns, a process encouraged by official policy.

Some two-thirds of the entire population is engaged in
livestock herding. The bovine herds are most heavily

concentrated in the regions of greatest rainfall along the
Senegal River from south of Brakna, Guidimaka, the Hodh
Occidental, and south of the Hodh Oriental. The concentration
diminishes as the 200-mm. zone is approached in the Northeast Trarza, to the center of the Hodh Oriental in the far
eastern part of the country. (See map.) The goat and sheep
population overlaps the bovine regions in the more northerly
reaches and is particularly concentrated in the triangle bounded
by M'Bout and Konkossa in the south and Tidjikja in the center
of the country. Goats and sheep are also numerous in the
Western Trarza and the Hodh. Camels are found mainly in
the regions of less than 200-mm. rainfall and east of the line
starting 200 km. north of Nema to Fort Trinquet in the far
north.

There are three types of livestock herding that affect the
degree of nomadism. First, there is the nomadism, entitled
transhumance, of lower Mauritania (Sahelien region). Here
the tribal camps are relatively stable, with good pastures and
predominantly bovine herds. The herds and people move to
different zones and even across national boundaries (Mauritania
and Mali), along fixed routes, and according to established
pattern in order to take advantage of seasonal vegetation growth.
Because the animals in this form of culture leave the inundated
and unhealthy zones during the winter rainy period, they are
generally healthier than livestock belonging to the sedentary
people. The dispersion of the animals also inhibits the trans-
mittal of contagious diseases. It is not unusual in this form
of nomadism to find schools and wells in the more important
camps, as well as some cultivation of the soil.

The second form of nomadism occurs in central Mauritania
(Adrar-Tagant), where movements are more erratic and dependent on rainfall. Sheep and camels go south with the advent
of the humid season and return north with the autumn rains.
Movements of people and herds are over greater distances but
are less regular than in the south. Third, there are the nomads
of the north, who can depend on no regular seasonal rainfall
and who travel with their camels, often over 1,000 km., in
search of pasture. The numbers of people involved are small,
and they are widely dispersed.

The sedentary zones are in the far south; the population
in this area maintains cattle and produces crops, principally
millet and sorghum. In addition to the various Negro ethnic
groups identified earlier, the sedentary zones include a number
of villages inhabited mainly by black Moors. The sedentary
population also includes the inhabitants of the oases in various

parts of the arid regions. Most of the sedentary population is
situated in the area along the Senegal River, which has the
highest population density in the country.

The social structure of the sedentary tribes is like that
of the Moorish tribes. Among the Moors, the principal unit
is the tribe, an ancient social organism composed of a number
of family groups or tents under a single chief, with common
traditions and habits. In its classic form, the tribe consists
of noble families at the top of the structure, either warriors
or marabouts (learned and religious castes); tributary groups
of shepherds and farmers, usually of Berber origin; artisans;
and haratines, who were subject peoples and many of whom
are now the black Moors who engage in sedentary agriculture
and often still pay tribute.

With the increasing modernization of Mauritania, the
warrior castes have lost their importance. Members of this
class have tended to be absorbed into the police corps and the
army. The marabouts tend to become teachers and administra-
tors. The Moorish caste system does not necessarily imply
marked differences in material wealth between castes but,
rather, defines mutual obligations and privileges. The noble
families own little land, and the equalitarian nomadic tradition
places a premium on generosity.

Among the Negro tribes, the Toucouleurs are most numerous. They inhabit both the Mauritanian and Senegalese sides
of the river and frequently have family and property interests
in both countries. They too have hereditary noble families,
free productive classes, artisans, and servant classes. The
Peuls are spread all over the valley and are only partly sedentary, since large numbers leave the villages during the
seasons of transhumance to follow the cattle.

A complicated system of land tenure and usage exists in
the flood plain of the Senegal River. There are numerous
examples of collective ownership, individual rights to use
land, and sharecroppers involving both Moors and the Negro
tribes.[4] No cadastral survey exists, and the system of tenure
is only known for certain limited parts of the valley. It is
evident that efforts to modernize agricultural production will
have to include a study of land ownership and rights.

Attempts to spread and improve education have been
severely hampered by the wide dispersion of the population
and the limited resources produced by a primitive livestock
and agricultural economy. The primary-school population
(ages 6-12) may be estimated at some 20 per cent of the total.
The percentage of children of primary-school age in school is

less than 10 per cent, although primary education absorbs 11
per cent of the total budget. The percentage of children in
school also varies widely depending on population concentration. Thus, 24 per cent are in school in the north around Port-
Etienne, but only about 4 per cent are in school in the Hodh
Oriental. The per pupil cost of primary education in Mauritania
(Francs de la Communauté Financière Africaine [CFAF]
21,000) in 1966 was well above the average for the other
French states of Africa (CFAF 9,700).

The generally harsh climatic conditions, the limited
amount of arable land, the great dispersion of the bulk of the
population, and the traditional social structure constitute serious limiting factors for the process of economic development.
The dissemination of modern technology and the extension of
central administration are made difficult by the widely scattered
population. Not only is land communication primitive, but
expensive improvements are difficult to justify in economic
terms, given the present level of production.

NOTES

1. For a more comprehensive analysis than will be presented here of Mauritania's political and social structure,
see Alfred G. Gerteiny, Mauritania (New York: Frederick A.
Praeger, 1967). Also see Genevieve Désiré-Vuillemin, Contribution à l'Histoire de la Mauritanie 1900-1934 (Dakar: Edi-
tions Clairafrique, 1962).

2. Gerteiny, op. cit., pp. 88-89. Peuls are also called
Fulbe, and Toucouleurs are also referred to as Halphoolaren.

3. République Islamique de Mauritanie (RIM), Ministère
des Finances, du Plan, et de la Fonction Publique, SEDES
(Société d'Etuder Pour la Développement Economique et
Sociale), Enquête Démographique 1964-1965: Généralités,
Méthodologie, Résultats Provisoires (October, 1966). In
1962, the population was estimated at 880,000. Mauritanian
authorities estimate the 1969 population at 1,140,000.

4. For a discussion of land-tenure arrangements in the
valley, see J. L. Boutillier et al., La Moyenne Vallée du
Sénégal, "Publication of the French Senegalese and Mauritanian
Republics" (1962), pp. 111-27.

2

THE STRUCTURE

OF

THE ECONOMY

THE MODERN SECTOR

The outstanding feature of the Mauritanian economy is its strong dual character. On the one hand, there are the traditional livestock and agricultural sectors, which for most yield little more than subsistence standards of living and in which about 90 per cent of the population is engaged. On the other hand, there is the modern sector in the northwestern part of the country, consisting of an iron mine, a copper mine nearing completion, and a developing fishing industry.

These enterprises are, in reality, foreign enclaves, developed with foreign capital and staffed at the higher levels almost entirely by Europeans. As extensions of the modern industrialized world, these industries are subject to cyclical variations in demand characteristic of their parent industries, as the sharp decline in iron-ore prices has demonstrated in recent years. The question of the profitability of these enterprises is important, for the government is entitled to a large share of the profits of the ore companies. The government also has a large share in the fish-processing facilities. Here, however, serious overinvestment in the past raises a question with respect to potential returns.

By their very nature, the enclave industries of the north can only have a limited direct influence on the process of introducing modern technology to the traditional sector. In the first place, these industries, whether in mineral extraction or in fish processing, are highly capital intensive in structure.

11

They will, therefore, employ small, but relatively skilled, local cadres. The specialized training required for these cadres will be largely provided by the industries themselves and will be of a nature not readily transferable to the traditional livestock and agricultural sectors. Even in fishing, where scope exists to develop a Mauritanian fishing fleet, the total requirement for manpower to man boats over the next decade is not expected to exceed 1,200.

Second, aside from the limited direct employment, income, and training effects of the enclave industries, their primary contribution to the development of the traditional sectors will be indirect, in the form of taxes and royalties on output and salaries and possible profit on operations that will accrue to the current government budget. This source of income already accounts for over one-fourth of total government current revenues. The possible impact of this source of revenue on the development effort in general should not be exaggerated. As will be shown, revenues from such sources will not rise significantly until 1973, the end of the second plan period. The copper mines are not expected to make an important contribution until 1975, when its share may amount to some 10 per cent of present government current revenues. Thus, the government's financial situation, even with a large contribution from the export of iron ore, remains critically tight.

Although revenues more than doubled between 1961 and 1969--initially because of the Mines de Fer de Mauritanie (MIFERMA) and later because of indirect tax yields--the budgetary balance on current accounts has been maintained by keeping current outlays in check and certainly below the level of pressing demands in the fields of rural services, social services, and maintenance. Less stringency has been applied to relatively lower-priority security and education expenses.

Finally, the enclaves can have an important, although limited, economic impact in providing markets for the output of domestically produced products. The market potential of the mining and fishing centers of Port-Etienne, Fort-Gouraud, and in the future Akjoujt, with their relatively high-salaried European and local staffs, have been only partially exploited by the vegetable growers of Atar and Chinguetti in the north and not at all by the livestock industry of the south and east. The opportunity exists to replace presently imported foodstuffs with domestically produced vegetables and meat once production, distribution, and marketing are properly organized. In this connection, the new government administrative center at

Nouakchott offers similar marketing possibilities to domestic
producers of agricultural products.

With a population of some 1 million persons, the potentially
active population (ages 15-60) is estimated to be some 600,000
(less than half male), of whom an estimated 400,000 are engaged in livestock herding and 160,000 in agriculture. The
proportion of the population under 15 years of age is 40-45
per cent of the total; the proportion over 60 is, therefore,
quite small. In fact, a good part of the female population in
the active age group should not be considered as part of the
labor force--i.e., willing and able to work--since traditional
social custom generally relegates the female to a quite passive
work role in the nomadic part of the population. These atti-
tudes are carried over to the modern sector, where relatively
few females participate in the labor force, constituting about
10 per cent of modern-sector employment.

Employment in the modern sector was estimated at
20,000 persons in 1968, half of whom were in the private sector. Foreigners constituted 30 per cent of private-sector employment and 10 per cent of public-sector employment and
dominate the higher managerial and professional jobs. In
general, the modern sector employs some 3 per cent of the
potential labor force. The absolute numbers employed
declined through 1965, as a result of the completion of major
iron-mining investments, and have risen slightly since.

Some 96 per cent of the private modern-sector labor
force is concentrated in the northern part of the country, principally in Nouakchott, Zouerate, and Port-Etienne. If public
employment (excluding the armed forces) is added, the north
contains an estimated 60 per cent of total employment in the
modern sector. Thus, modern-sector employment affects a
very small part of the population. It is fairly stable in numbers and is subject, as will be shown, to great shifts in types
of occupation. Finally, the productive part of the modern
sector is heavily concentrated in the most sparsely populated
part of the country, where its higher incomes and modern
skills can have but a minimal influence on the bulk of the traditional sector.

The difference between the modern and the traditional
sectors is even more clearly seen from the figures on income
distribution. National-accounts estimates are available for
1959, 1964, and 1968; the accounts have been revised period-
ically, and details for some years are better than others. [1]
These figures are most imprecise in imputing value added to
the traditional sector and most reliable in estimating for the

modern sector.   They are, nevertheless, probably reliable
enough to give a general impression of the relative importance
of the main sectors that contribute to the national product.

Total wages and salaries in the modern private sector in
1964 are estimated at CFAF 5. 4 billion.   Total private employment amounted to 9, 300, of whom some 33 per cent were
foreigners (both African and European).   The foreigners held
the great majority of executive and skilled positions.   In the
two highest classes of wage and salary earners, foreigners
held 94 per cent of the positions and earned 50 per cent of all
wage and salary payments.   In general, Mauritanians held
two-thirds of the jobs in the modern private sector but received only one-third of the total wage and salary payments. [2]
It is estimated that foreigners habitually transfer over 50 per
cent of their income abroad.   In 1964, it is estimated that
such transfers amounted to some CFAF 4. 8 billion.   By 1967,
foreigners held 91 per cent of the positions in the top two
categories.

Employment in the public sector amounted to about 8, 200
persons in 1964, and total wage and salary payments amounted
to CFAF 4. 1 billion.   Foreigners were estimated to constitute
some 10 per cent of public-sector employment in 1964 and in
1968, when such employment rose to an estimated 10, 500.   A
large number of foreigners in the public service receive most
of their remuneration from technical assistance programs
paid by other countries (mainly France) and international
organizations.   The income produced per capita in the modern
sector may be roughly estimated to exceed that of the traditional
sector by some ten times on the average.   If foreign workers
are excluded, Mauritanian income per worker in the modern
sector may be estimated at five times that of the traditional
sector.

The figures on the distribution of the gross domestic
product (GDP) at market prices in 1968 indicate that the traditional sector produces some 40 per cent of the total; mining
and construction, 35 per cent; and commerce, services, and
the public sector, the balance.   Thus, the bulk of the working
force is engaged in producing less than half the domestic
product.   Moreover, the large proportion of the gross national
product (GNP) produced in the mining sector is offset by heavy
factor payments abroad by the enterprise producing the iron
ore, as well as by considerable transfer payments by the
foreign workers who receive the greatest part of private-sector
wage and salary payments.   The sum of factor payments and
transfers abroad by enterprises and wage and salary earners

was estimated at CFAF 8.1 billion in 1968. GNP was accordingly estimated at CFAF 39.0 billion, compared with a GDP of CFAF 47.1 billion in 1968.

LIVESTOCK

The livestock herds of Mauritania represent the greatest resource of the country's traditional sector, as well as the principal occupation of the bulk of its people. Livestock contributed an estimated CFAF 13 billion to the GDP in 1968, or some 25 per cent of total GDP; the entire agricultural sector including livestock produced a GDP of about CFAF 16 billion. [3] There are an estimated 2 million head of cattle, 6 million sheep and goats, 700,000 camels, and 300,000 horses and asses in Mauritania.

The principal factors limiting the development of livestock are the quantity and quality of pastures, the availability of drinking water, and the pathology and sanitary condition of the animals. In general, animals in the drier zones are healthier and less subject to disease than those in the moister regions. As indicated earlier, the increased concentration of animals under transhumance in the south during the dry season causes a deterioration in health conditions and in the quality of pasture due to overgrazing. In addition, vast areas cannot be used in a rational manner to pasture the herds because of the absence of drinking water for man and beast during a large part of the year.

These conditions over the centuries have produced a breed of animal under transhumance particularly adapted to the terrain. In effect, the animals are subject to alternating periods of famine and feast. They often go two or three days without water during the long marches between pastures. The African Zebu cattle are of two distinct types--the Moorish Zebu and the lower-yielding Peul Zebu. This is the only type of animal able to survive the natural climatic conditions of the country, as well as to resist the epizootic diseases that afflict animals in the more temperate zones, although even the Zebu can benefit greatly from sanitary protective measures.

Under these conditions, it is not surprising that the productivity of the animals is less than that of herds in more favorable climates. Nevertheless, despite the regular deprivation of food and water to which they are subject, the herds survive, reproduce, and nourish a human population, while

leaving an important surplus for export. The limited knowledge of the physiology of the African Zebu makes it difficult
to crossbreed successfully with superior-yielding types of
animals. The natural conditions of the country, together with
the physiology of the Zebu, makes it impossible to apply
European or American coefficients of converting fodder into
meat and milk.

Cows do not reach maturity until after the fifth year, and
do not become fertile until the third year. The birthrate
rarely exceeds 60 per cent and the rate of survival is 50 per
cent. Beef cattle in the traditional livestock culture are
marketed young, often yielding less than 300 kg. on the hoof
and returning less than 50 per cent per carcass. Meat and
milk yields are correspondingly low for sheep and cows. Virtually all of the milk is consumed by the herders, thereby de-
priving the young calves of adequate nourishment and leading
to high mortality rates. Accordingly, the annual rates of off-
take as a percentage of total herds is estimated at 8 per cent
for cows, 30 per cent for sheep and goats, and 5 per cent for
camels.

In addition to the low rates of return, the system of distribution and marketing of livestock is unmechanized. At
maturity, the animals are sold on consignment, usually against
an advance, at the major livestock centers--particularly
Kaedi, Kiffa, and Nema--to middlemen, who drive them
through Senegal, where they are fattened en route to markets
in Dakar. It is a system in which a large degree of trust
exists between herder and merchant. The merchant, or
middleman, sells the cattle at the market in Dakar and then
pays the herder.

The provisionment of the Dakar market is irregular, since
the herders come into contact with the sedentary settled areas
during only one part of the transhumance cycle. During these
contacts, a system of barter of animals for grain and other
products also takes place. In general, the herder is dependent
on middlemen and the vagaries of a market that is from 500
to 1,000 km. from the collection points in Mauritania. Yet,
the system nevertheless yields returns to Mauritanian herders
that compare favorably with the experience of other African
livestock-raising areas.

CROP AGRICULTURE

Millet-Sorghum

The main crop produced in Mauritania is millet and a close relative, sorghum. Output is estimated at some 110,000 tons a year. Three types of culture are identifiable. The first and by far the most important type (culture de décrue), accounting for some three-fourths of total output, is represented by farming in the flood plain of the Senegal River and its tributaries. The millet is planted in areas (the oualo) where the river flood has receded. Some 40 per cent of flood-plain output is in the Brakna/Gorgol region, and 15 per cent is in the Guidimaka regions of the river. The yield is an estimated 400 kg. per hectare.

The low returns are due to the use of traditional techniques of cultivation; the irregularity of the flood, which can double in area from one year to another; and the general inadequacy of water, given the techniques of cultivation. Planting usually takes place late, in March and April, after the ground has already lost a considerable amount of moisture. The ground is not tilled; a forked stick is used to make a hole into which the seed is inserted. The growth of the plant is entirely dependent on the remaining moisture in the ground, which is considerably diminished by the hot dry winds that blow from the east starting in April and May.

The second type of millet-sorghum culture is that dependent on rainfall. Average yields are about 300 kg. per hectare. In Guidimaka, where rainfall is some 500 mm. a year, yields are higher. The crop is planted, with the same techniques described above, at the first rainfall. Occasionally, a second crop may be obtained, depending on the amount of rainfall. The principal limitations on this type of culture, aside from technique, are the irregularity of annual rainfall and the general lack of adequate moisture, which are further accentuated by a rapid evaporation rate.

The third type of millet-sorghum culture concerns largely the nomadic herders and may be considered a secondary activity to their principal occupation of raising livestock. It is based on the brief periods of flood that follow the intense, but short, desert rainfalls. The collection of water in the wadis leaves enough moisture to produce a poor crop. In the last generation, a number of small dams were erected by the government and occasionally by local communities to retard the flow of the water and increase the inundated area.

The investment in these dams has yielded extremely low returns, although providing some crop supplement to the livestock output of the nomads, and a few sedentary villages in the pasturelands. Where the opportunity cost of labor is virtually nil, the increased output of millet, however meager, may be defensible on social grounds. The opportunity cost of capital is considerably higher, however, and it is on these grounds that the investment in dams of this type may be questioned.

The total domestic output of millet is insufficient to meet domestic consumption requirements. Accordingly, a gradually increasing quantity, in accordance with population growth, has been imported annually from Senegal and Mali, varying currently between 10,000 and 30,000 tons, depending on rainfall conditions and relative prices.

Dates

There are an estimated 1 million date-palm trees in Mauritania. They are concentrated in the oases of Adrar, Tagant, Assaba, and the Hodh. Annual production is estimated at 10,000 tons, which is apparently sufficient to cover domestic consumption needs. With few exceptions, date palms grow wild, without pruning or special care. Yields are accordingly low, and variations in quality are considerable.

Although adequate ground water appears to exist for irrigation in the main producing areas, the modern large-scale cultivation of dates is retarded by a number of factors. Principal among these is that it takes a tree about five years to bear fruit. With limited capital, few Mauritanians would wish to invest in plantation culture without return for such a long gestation period because they discount the future so heavily. In fact, the bulk of the trees are owned by a few absentee landlords whose principal occupation is livestock. They rent their trees for the annual output and collect whatever revenue this yields.

Other Crops

Small quantities of wheat, corn, rice, and other crops are grown in isolated areas. Demand for rice has been rising, and imports are estimated at some 12,000 tons annually. The cultivation of vegetables has begun in the oases of Atar and Chinguetti, while market gardening has started on a small scale near Nouakchott and Rosso. In general, great deficiencies exist in the production of vegetables, which results in low quality and high prices.

The output of gum arabic, which contributes some CFAF 350 million to the GDP annually and includes an export of 2,000 tons (value estimated at CFAF 100 million), is gradually diminishing because of the destructive cutting practices employed.

CONCLUSION

The economic impact of the modern sector on the rest of the economy is limited from the point of view of employment, domestic income generation, demand for local products, and the spreading of modern technology. In short, the modern sector in Mauritania produces little in the way of domestic external economies. Further, its contribution to current tax revenues, although a large percentage of the small government budget, is fixed by long-term conventions and, in any case, is insufficient to create an important amount of public savings that could be devoted to investment in the development of the rest of the economy.

The modern sector also absorbs a disproportionate share of current social-service expenditures, particularly for education. Accordingly, the problem facing the authorities concerned with development planning is how to improve the economic and social well-being of the bulk of the population, whose low productivity yields little more than minimum standards of living, given that the public sector does not have the current resources to make any significant impact on the general level of health, education, and other public services. In Part II, the performance of the economy will be examined in terms of the recent experience in confronting this as well as other problems.

NOTES

1. République Islamique de Mauritanie (RIM), Ministère de la Planification et du Développement Rural, Comptes Economiques de la République Islamique de Mauritanie (1968).

2. RIM, <u>Bulletin Statistique et Economique,</u> No. 8 (1965).

3. See Richard M. Westebbe, <u>Mauritania: Guidelines for a Four-Year Development Program</u> (Washington, D.C.: International Bank for Reconstruction and Development, 1968), Tables 22-23, for a detailed estimate of rural-sector GDP in 1964, with projections through 1971.

II

RECENT
ECONOMIC
PERFORMANCE

3

THE FIRST PLAN, 1963-66

The first serious attempt at national planning began in 1962 and culminated in a four-year plan, 1963-66. Since the approval of the National Assembly was not obtained until July, 1963, the effective dates of the plan were adjusted to cover the period June, 1963-June, 1967. Detailed figures on funds committed and spent are only available for the first three years of the plan. In any event, after the end of 1966, the plan ceased to be a practical instrument for guiding development policy.

The government decided to use 1967 as a year of reassessment and preparation for a new four-year plan, an exercise that, in practice, extended to 1970. In order to assist in this endeavor, the International Bank for Reconstruction and Development (IBRD), or World Bank, at the request of the government, sent a technical assistance mission to Mauritania for three months in spring, 1967. (The report of the mission is available.)

The plan was based on two fundamental objectives, from which follow its more specific objectives: to reduce the country's dependence on foreign financing and on foreign personnel and to prepare the basis for a subsequent development program beginning in 1967 and designed to promote the welfare of the entire nation. [1]

The first objective was to be accomplished by a policy of "draconic" austerity in public expenditures, coupled with fiscal reforms to increase revenues, leading to an elimination of the existing budget deficit. Adequate credits were to be provided for maintaining the stock of national capital while a proper investment budget was being established. A program of systematic training and placement of personnel, based on a census of needs at all levels, was to be undertaken in order to reduce the dependence on foreign resources while providing for the increasing demand for trained cadres that would increase the absorptive capacity for investment.

The second objective of preparing the base for the future economic and social development of the country was to be accomplished, in part, by a series of basic studies of the nation's human and material resources, which would enable the objectives of the second plan to be quantified. In addition, a program of basic infrastructure investments was envisaged in roads, communications, schools, and hospitals, including the stimulation of regional poles of development.

In the livestock sector, sanitation, water projects, and capital-intensive processing and commercialization facilities were projected. In agriculture, major dependence was placed on pilot hydroagricultural works. Social investments were to be limited to the minimum. Encouragement was to be given to the establishment of small Mauritanian manufacturing and service enterprises to tie together the public services, the big enterprises, and the traditional sectors.

The plan did not, by and large, achieve its aims in terms of the stated fundamental objectives. With respect to the objective of reducing Mauritania's dependence on external finance, the government in 1963 renounced the French current budget subsidies and simultaneously introduced an austerity budget designed to enforce a balance of current expenditures with revenues. Basically, the reform of the fiscal system envisaged by the plan did not occur, and most of the increased receipts resulted from the coming into operation of the MIFERMA iron mines. Even the allocation of budgetary resources, as will be discussed more fully later, was often made on grounds other than their likely contribution to economic development.

The draconic economies proposed by the plan were effected on high-priority outlays, such as maintenance expenditures, which were reduced so much that existing capital was allowed to deteriorate. The investment budget remained little more than a collection of residual items that could not be covered in the current budget and that could be paid out of special supplementary grants from the French government. The bulk of the investment program was financed by French and EEC grants.

By the end of the plan period, only limited progress had

been made in replacing expatriates with Mauritanians. The
census of human resource requirements that was to have been
the basis for a systematic program of training and replace-
ments was never carried out. Because of the limited progress
in "Mauritanizing" the public services and because of the rising
need for trained personnel, the number of foreign technical
personnel provided by the programs of technical assistance
has remained approximately constant. In a number of fields,
there are not enough technically trained people, either expatriates or Mauritanians, to perform the work required.

The second fundamental objective of the plan was the preparation of the basis for general economic and social development during the second plan period. This was to be accomplished
mainly by the completion of certain fundamental studies, as well
as by a program of infrastructure investments. The program of
studies was based on the quite reasonable proposition that national planning was impossible in the face of an almost total lack
of knowledge about the country's demography, family consumption habits, commerce, surface and subsurface resources, and
rural production.

In fact, the only statistical study accomplished, at least
in part, was that done by SEDES on demography. The results
of a pilot inquiry undertaken in 1962 were published in 1964.
This was followed by a more general demographic survey in
1964-65, the provisional results of which were published in
October, 1966.[2] This study is being revised, and a complete
census will be undertaken at an unspecified later time. Financing has not yet been obtained for the family budget study, while
the study of interior and exterior commerce has been postponed
until the second plan.

A modest program of geological aerial surveys and geological mapping was included in the plan. This program is largely
on schedule and has resulted in some interesting indications
of mineral deposits (beryllium, chrome, fluorite). In view of
the extent of area to be surveyed, the sums projected by the
plan were not large. No detailed studies exist of agricultural
land resources. There are also no reliable statistics on output in the agricultural and livestock sectors. In general, the
basic knowledge of the country's people and resources at the
beginning of the second plan period leaves a good deal to be
desired.

Allocation of Resources

The plan projected total investments of CFAF 27.8 billion
for the four-year period, of which CFAF 13.6 billion were in
the public sector and CFAF 14.2 billion were in the private
sector. (See Appendix Table 1.) About one-third of total investments were allocated to mining; these were almost equally
divided between iron ore at Zouerate and copper at Akjoujt.
Urban development, both regional and in the main centers,
was to account for 15 per cent of total investments. A further
12 per cent was for transport and communications infrastructure
and equipment, and only 9 per cent was for the rural sector
(agriculture and livestock). Studies were allocated less than
6 per cent of total investment.

In terms of planning in Mauritania, total investment can
be little more than an indicative concept. The planning authorities and government, in fact, can directly influence only the
public sector. Although 60 per cent of private-sector investment was estimated to be in mining and the government has a
substantial role to play in granting concessions and negotiating
the terms of operating conventions, the basic decisions to
exploit the deposits, as well as the bulk of the capital required,
belong to private foreigners. Close to one-quarter of public
investment was allocated to transport and communications
infrastructure and an almost equal amount to urban development.

Rural production received 17 per cent of which half went
to several capital-intensive hydroagricultural projects. Of
the balance allocated to the pastoral sector, about two-thirds
was for the construction and maintenance of rural wells and
about one-third for refrigerator plants and abattoirs. A small
sum was set aside for immunization parks. Training and
education was to receive only 6.7 per cent of public investment,
of which half was for secondary, general, and technical education; a small share was for vocational training. The maritime
fishing industry based on Port-Etienne was allocated some 7
per cent of total public investment.

A review of the allocation of public investment indicates
that close to half, including a large part of investment devoted
to transport and communications infrastructure and urban
development, was not oriented in accordance with productive
criteria. In the case of transport and communications infrastructure, studies indicate that only the Rosso-Nouakchott
road may be considered to have an economic justification in
terms of present and potential freight tonnage. Similarly, the

wharf at Nouakchott and the port facilities at Port-Etienne may
be justified by the role assigned to these ports as centers of
national economic activity. The plan document sets forth
expenditures by project that are evaluated neither by rate of
return nor by their place in a national pattern of mutually
complementary investments. Urban development may well
have some justification in a program of development, although
it would be difficult to defend insofar as it induced untimely
rural to urban migration and contributed to urban land speculation.

Although such investments may well be justified for other
reasons relating to the establishment of a new state, it must
be recognized that they involve large recurrent and maintenance
expenditures. These expenditures will compete in the future
for resources that might otherwise have been devoted to investment. In Mauritania, the rising requirement for maintenance expenditures, as indicated earlier, has not been met,
and existing investments have been allowed to deteriorate.
The large amounts devoted to infrastructure investment resulted
from the assumption made by the planners that such investment
was a necessary precondition to economic development.

The rural sector--livestock and agriculture--contains
over 90 per cent of the population, which exists on close to
minimum levels of subsistence. In the case of agriculture,
primary emphasis was placed on highly capital-intensive
projects on the grounds that such projects could serve as
models for future, more general development of agriculture.
In fact, a good deal has been learned by French aid agencies
of the limitations of irrigation works, as well as the possibilities of achieving satisfactory returns. The analysis of
this sector assumed, on the basis of inadequate information
available, that the ecological production limits had been
reached in the traditional cultivation of millet and sorghum.
Since then, pilot projects and experiments have demonstrated
that substantial increases in output could be obtained with
relatively small investments and simple changes in technology.

In livestock, it was apparently assumed that fundamental
changes in the system of commercializing meat would be one
important way to improve the standard of living of the herders.
This led to decisions to construct capital-intensive refrigerator plants and abattoirs. In fact, as is now recognized, the
returns on investment in animal hygiene and in providing wells
are far greater and do not lead to a rise in costs of production
in order to supply the limited markets for processed meat.

In summary, the plan may be said to have been based in

large part on three conceptions that are no longer valid. First, it was not oriented toward increasing output but, rather, emphasized investments that either inherently involved no rate of return or, at least after the fact, cannot be justified in terms of any rational calculation of returns. Second, the basic assumptions with respect to the productive possibilities in the traditional sectors containing the bulk of the population were not well founded. Not only did this lead to too low a share of investment funds being allocated to these sectors, but even the funds provided can be considered to have been to a great extent misallocated. No doubt the conceptions with respect to the production possibilities in livestock and agriculture also influenced the programs of technical training for these sectors. Third, the plan did not adequately provide for widening the scope for profitable investments that could be undertaken in the future. The program of projected studies was limited, and the program for training the personnel needed to enable new investments to be undertaken and manned was inadequate.

General Results of the Plan

Figures on the outcome of the plan are available for the first four years, through June 30, 1967. These are summarized in Table 1. The outcome of the plan may be viewed in terms of disbursements and commitments. The plan called for CFAF 27.8 billion of outlays, and, in fact, CFAF 26.7 billion were disbursed. Commitments for financing amounted to CFAF 33.8 billion.[3] (See Appendix Tables 2 and 3 for a detailed breakdown of private- and public-sector plan provisions, disbursements, and commitments.)

The fishing sector accounted for nearly CFAF 3.9 billion of the excess of private and public commitments over plan provisions, a phenomena that is discussed more fully later. In mining, both disbursements and commitments exceeded plan provisions by some CFAF 2.1 billion. This sector was dominated by the MIFERMA iron mines, which experienced greatly increased costs in relation to the amounts originally foreseen as necessary. The Akjoujt copper mines, which were included in the plan provisions, did not get under way at all during the plan period.

An excess of some CFAF 700 million occurred in transport and communications infrastructure. Most of this excess came about because more money was borrowed for the Rosso-Nouakchott road and less was disbursed than was planned.

TABLE 1

Plan Investment Projections and Outcome,
July 1, 1963-June 30, 1967,
by Category

Nature of Investment	Plan Provisions	Disburse-ments	Commit-ments	Per Cent of Plan Provisions*
	Million (CFAF)			
General studies	1,581	580	864	36.7
Transport & com-munications infra-structure	3,348	2,376	4,038	71.1
Agriculture & livestock	2,400	1,283	1,865	53.5
Mining	9,380	11,555	11,555	123.2
Fishing	1,910	4,080	5,751	213.6
Education & training	922	393	869	42.6
Health & hygiene	770	804	932	104.4
Urban infrastructure & housing	4,023	2,362	4,214	58.7
Administrative buildings	2,147	1,175	1,639	54.7
Services	1,270	2,099	2,106	165.3
Total	27,751	26,707	33,834	96.2

*Disbursements divided by plan provisions.

Note: In Appendix Tables 1 and 2 (see pp. 135 & 136), plan provisions for public transport and communications infrastructure differ by CFAF 3 millions and public education and training by CFAF 1/2 million. The differences result from unexplained changes between the 1963 plan document and the Bilan (balance sheet) published in 1967.

Source: RIM, Bilan d'Exécution Plan Quadriennal, 1963-66 (Nouakchott, 1967).

Bids received for the road indicate that the final cost may be
below the amount foreseen by international lending agencies.
The wharf of Nouakchott was completed at a final estimated
cost of some CFAF 170 million above the amount provided in
the plan.   Public expenditures and commitments for services
exceeded plan provisions by some CFAF 340 million, and those
by the private sector, by some CFAF 500 million.   Details are
lacking for this category, which may, in part, concern state
participation in mixed companies.

On the basis of disbursements, plan targets were not
achieved in the categories of general studies, transport and
communications infrastructure, agriculture and livestock,
education and training, urban infrastructure and housing, and
administrative buildings.   In some sectors, such as fishing
and mining, poor planning and unforeseen cost increases led
to commitments and disbursements higher than those planned.
In the rural sector, not enough money was available.   Lack of
experienced personnel and of an efficient mechanism for trans-
lating programs into projects constituted an obstacle to plan
implementation.   The failure to produce basic studies created
a serious obstacle for future planning.

In general, although total private and public disbursements
of some CFAF 26. 7 billion took place, compared with a projected amount of CFAF 27. 8 billion in the four-year period,
actual expenditures for the MIFERMA iron-mine complex and
the fishing industry exceeded estimated costs substantially.
The public-sector investments in the plan were, in many cases,
delayed by the failure to obtain foreign financing.   A number
of investments, included in disbursements, were undertaken
outside the plan, particularly in airports, secondary roads,
public buildings, livestock hygiene, public enterprises, and
government participation in enterprises.   Private investments
in MIFERMA and in the fishing industry amounted to 70 per
cent of total private investment in the first four years.   Private
investment, in turn, constituted about 50 per cent of total investment disbursements.   Investment disbursements in rural
production (agriculture, livestock, forests) accounted for only
5 per cent of the total and about 16 per cent of total public investment disbursements.   In the ensuing discussion of the
various sectors, important details with respect to specific
projects and programs will be set forth.

Plan Administration

When the plan was published in 1963, provision was made
to place it under a commissioner general in the Office of the
President responsible for the administrative services and
consultative agencies dealing with the elaboration, application,
and control of the plan, except for specific tasks relegated to
the appropriate ministries. The plan organization was to take
its authority directly from the highest office in the country,
since the importance of the plan as the "engine of development"
was such that it influenced the political situation, and the organization would be required to arbitrate between the different
sectors of national economic activity.

The organization was shifted in 1965 to the Ministry of
Finance and, in late 1966, to the Ministry of Foreign Affairs.
The organization had no authority to coordinate the development activities of the various parts of the government, nor
could it supervise the execution of projects. Even the process
of studying, gaining approval, and finding finances for new
projects often escaped its control, since individual ministries
frequently deal directly with higher authorities and external
sources of financing. Finally, the organization was inadequately
staffed to perform real planning functions. There were neither
qualified personnel to draw up new plans, which involves ex-
amining the alternatives and selecting the optimum way of using
scarce resources to achieve objectives, nor people capable of
evaluating the economic impact of programs under way.

The organization consisted of three experienced senior
expatriate officials, plus a director and a deputy appointed in
1967. One senior official translated the projects proposed by
individual ministries into requests for foreign financing. This
was a coordinating and negotiation function, which was particularly important because virtually all financing comes from
Fonds d'Aide et de Coopération (FAC) and the Fonds Europeens
de Développement (FED). A second senior official supervised
and controlled expenditures for projects financed by FAC and
FED and reported to these organizations. His presence was a
necessary condition to receiving financing from these agencies.
A third senior official was director of the government's
Statistical Service, which was only indirectly related to the
functions of a planning agency. This service was understaffed
and underfinanced and, therefore, unable to provide adequate
current statistics, let alone develop the data needed for plan
formulation and revision.

Given its recent history, lack of authority, and lack of

personnel, it is not surprising that the plan organization was
unable to perform its function. A review of the experience of
the first four years of the plan indicates that projects selected
were not carefully and competently studied, even when foreign
contractors and consulting firms were involved. This led not
only to widespread delays in execution but has also been responsible for costs greatly exceeding estimates in a significant
number of cases. Projects were not ranked according to their
rates of return but, in some cases, were undertaken as if the
funds involved were virtually a free good.

Little was done in the way of long-term sector programing.
Accordingly, it was difficult, if not impossible, to establish
rational development objectives or to relate what was being
done in one sector with that in another. Finally, no procedure
existed for annual reviews of plan results or for a coordination
of annual budget policy with plan requirements. With no effective coordination of development programs under way,
government supervision and control was spotty and, at times,
nonexistent. The loss to the national economy because of delays, excessive costs, and nonviable projects was great.

The IBRD technical assistance mission placed great stress
on the reorganization of the plan organization, together with
the creation of a coordinating and sector-programing apparatus
in the government. [4] This mission suggested that the Office of
the Economic and Financial Adviser to the President be combined with that of the head of a new national planning agency in
the Office of the President. Instead, the government at the
Third People's Party Congress of January, 1968, announced
a reorganization of the various ministries, including the
creation of a new Ministry of Planning and Rural Development,
in order to carry out the objectives of the second plan, which
are largely based on the IBRD mission's report.

The new ministry is headed by the former Presidential
economic adviser. It will be responsible for plan and development program formulation, control, and financing. Particular
stress is placed on the rural sector, in that all the agricultural
and livestock services of the government come under the new
ministry. An internal coordinating mechanism was established
within the new ministry. Further, an interministerial programing committee has been established, including the Ministry
of Finance. A committee of Cabinet economic ministers will
meet regularly to discuss planning and economic policy issues.
The new minister has announced his intentions of working for
the full coordination of the annual budget with future annual
plans.

So far, the planning staff of the ministry has drafted the new four-year plan, which became operational in early 1970. The staff was augmented by one expatriate economist, and further additions are anticipated. The Ministry of Planning and Rural Development contains the following services related to planning: a planning service, an external-aid service, and an expenditure-control service, as well as a service for statistics and studies. This organization corresponds closely to the recommendations of the IBRD mission. It is too early to make any evaluation of the operation of the new organization. Much will depend on the degree of success that the new ministry will have in solving staffing problems.

THE SECOND PLAN, 1970-73

After 1968, the strategy of development recommended by the IBRD technical assistance mission of 1967 was adopted as the basis for a "Mauritanian Road to Development." The Third People's Party Congress of January, 1968, in Nouakchott confirmed this decision. The years between 1967 and 1970, in effect, became years of transition between the first and second plans. The delay did not mean that no progress was being made toward improving decision-making and achieving development objectives. With an agreed-upon strategy--focused on the rural sector and elaborated on in some detail, project by project--the new Ministry of Planning and Rural Development had a basis for its work.

The annual plan exercise was one positive step toward better coordinating the key budgetary spending decisions with development requirements. In 1969, agreement was reached on setting up a new budgetary coordinating committee consisting of the President, the Minister of Planning and Rural Development, and the Minister of Finance as permanent members. Other ministers would be invited to attend, as appropriate. The committee was designated to evaluate all proposals for budgetary spending in the light of the requirements for the annual plan presented by the Minister of Planning and Rural Development. It would be the mechanism for ensuring that development objectives were given proper consideration in relation to other national objectives.

During this period (1967-70), one deficiency that appeared concerned the authority of the Ministry of Planning and Rural Development. As one of a number of ministries, it could not

really play the role of superministry. It depended for its
success on the authority of the President, who, in Mauritania,
is the only one who can finally reconcile conflicting views
within the government. A further problem arose with respect
to the interministerial programing committee. While con-
ceptually sound, the committee did not work well, because the
various ministries did not have sufficient trained personnel to
do competent staff work. Accordingly, the committee could
not effectively coordinate government programs, nor could it
provide the kind of evaluation of specific proposals and do the
studies that the ministers needed. Realizing that time would
be needed to create a trained senior staff, the Ministry of
Planning and Rural Development took steps to set up a Central
Study Bureau in the Plan Directorate, where scarce available
local and expatriate technical talent could be concentrated.

Aside from problems connected with the scarcity of trained
people and difficulties in coordination, the new plan was delayed because of a basic political decision to consult the people.
It was felt that the lack of resources would require hard choices
to be made. An exercise was accordingly started, designed to
inform the people of the real choices and to get their approval
for the priorities selected. For this purpose, regional commissions were set up, and questionnaires were sent to each
locality and party section asking what projects they wanted
and what financial contribution or contributions in kind they
were prepared to make. A basic purpose of the exercise was
to change the prevailing view that the central government is
the dispenser of all benefits and that national economic constraints are irrelevant. The process of discussing the demands of each region and the government's plans took a
considerable amount of time, although senior officials believe
that it was time well spent.

The regionalization of the plan followed from the creation
in 1968 of a new regional administrative structure, which replaced the former structures and their subdivisions. The new
regions were designed to create a more economically viable
grouping of localities. Each region has a governor and a deputy
for administration and economic affairs, as well as an elected
commission. The regional governments have their own budgets.
Their main sources of revenue are the head tax on cattle and
some license taxes. It will take some time before an evaluation
of the new structure is possible.

The desire to create a "mystique" of the plan is laudable.
Nevertheless, after all is said and done, the government will
have to make the hard choices, although, admittedly, it has

gained a clearer conception of demand at the local level and, therefore, of the parameters within which it can maneuver in carrying out planning.

The new plan is a modest document. It is a "plan cadre," which sets forth the basic sector goals that are to guide annual investment and budget programs for the four-year period. At the outset, it recognizes that precise projections are misleading, given the inadequacy of data; that external financing is not secured for most projects; and that firm spending plans can only be made annually in the light of the latest information and given available budgetary resources. Nevertheless, a list of priority projects is included for the plan period. The plan is quite realistic in recognizing the heavy dependence of the country on external financing, the amounts and patterns of which are not entirely subject to Mauritanian influence.

Three main obstacles to acquiring and using available foreign aid effectively are identified. First are the problems of recurring costs for maintenance and depreciation associated with every project. Unless funds are made available to cover recurrent costs, the benefits of infrastructure investment cannot be realized. Second, the new plan recognizes the lack of adequately trained people and the necessity of not undertaking projects that cannot be staffed. Third is the lack of studies. This deficiency plagued the previous plan. Projects have to be supported by adequate analysis of what they are intended to do. The document is quite candid in saying that foreign influence will be greater in making choices and establishing priorities "when we don't know exactly what we want."[5]

The new plan does not give full cost figures for all the projects proposed, nor does it contain an estimate of total public investments; however, a general estimate can be made of the approximate magnitudes that the priorities adopted indicate. (See Table 2.) The new plan apparently assumes a rate of development spending about twice that of the first plan. Given the inadequacies of that exercise and the substantial deviations in the pattern of spending compared with what was planned, it is not clear how meaningful such comparisons are. Yet, an annual rate of public investments of some CFAF 4 billion does not seem excessive when one notes that, in 1968, public development spending, excluding technical assistance, rose to some CFAF 3 billion. It is also not clear to what extent actual spending in any year will be influenced by past commitments and projects under way. Since a good deal of even the priority projects proposed are not yet ready for financing, there will no doubt be delays at least in the initial years.

TABLE 2

Estimated Public Plan Magnitudes, 1970-73
(CFAF billion)

	1963-67 (actual)		1970-73	
	Total	Per Cent	Total	Per Cent
Rural sector	2.0	24	7.0	41
Transport & communications	2.3	29	4.0	23
Health & education	1.4	16	2.0	12
Urban development	1.1	13	3.0	18
Public buildings	0.5	6	.5	3
Miscellaneous	1.0	12	.5	3
	8.3	100	17.0	100

Source: RIM, Deuxième Plan de Développement
Economique et Social, 1970-1973 (Nouakchott, 1970), p. 6.

Two major issues arise from a review of the new plan.
First, it includes projects of doubtful priority in terms of
economic returns. The proposed Nouakchott-Nema road may
well do a good deal to tie the nation together, but far higher
returns would be earned by improved transport links with the
populous agricultural zone along the Senegal River. Second,
as will be shown, a major constraint recognized by the plan
itself is the lack of local resources to support the recurrent
and local contribution required for projects financed with
foreign aid. This, then is a matter of the capacity of the
country to generate adequate current budget surpluses to
finance its share of investment spending after making adequate
provisions for the recurrent costs of new and past investments.
It would seem that high-priority attention will have to be given
to tax reforms and to pruning current expenditures if the new
plan is to be carried out successfully. There are grounds
for some optimism, since Mauritania has demonstrated its

capacity in the past to impose severe austerity criteria on
spending.

Aside from these reservations, the new plan represents
a realistic approach to the problems of achieving development.
It does not rely on meaningless and misleading aggregate projections of the main economic parameters within a mathemat-
ically consistent macroeconomic framework. There are too
many unknowns to do this and too little policy content in conclusions derived from such an exercise at this stage of the
country's development. The plan may also provide the basis
for widening the scope of development activities in the future
by increasing the number of productive investment alternatives.
This should occur as a result of the training of specialized
staffs able to plan and carry out projects and as a consequence
of the completion of studies that will increase knowledge of the
basic economic and social variables affecting development and
that will provide the basis for more and better projects. Foreign aid agencies, under these circumstances, will also find
an expanded basis for their operations in Mauritania in the
future.

NOTES

1. RIM, Plan Quadriennal de Développement Economique
et Social, 1963-1966 (Nouakchott, 1963).

2. RIM, Ministère des Finances, du Plan, et da la Fonction
Publique, SEDES, Enquête Démographique 1964-1965:
Généralités, Méthodologie, Résultats Provisoires (October,
1966).

3. In a review of the first three years of the plan, it was
noted that CFAF 1.3 billion of excess commitments were for
purposes not specified in the plan. The figures for the commitments for the four-year period should probably be similarly
qualified. See RIM, Bilan Plan Quadriennal 1963-1966 de 2
Années d'Exécution (Nouakchott, 1967).

4. Richard M. Westebbe, Mauritania: Guidelines for a
Four-Year Development Program (Washington, D.C.: IBRD,
1968), pp. 113-21.

5. RIM, Deuxième Plan de Développement Economique et
Social, 1970-1973 (Nouakchott, 1970), p. 6.

CHAPTER

4

**OUTPUT
INCOME
AND
EMPLOYMENT**

TRENDS IN GROSS OUTPUT

Between 1959 and 1968, Mauritania's GDP, at market prices, rose by an average annual rate of 12.5 per cent in current prices, from CFAF 16.4 billion to CFAF 47.1 billion. Given price increases during this period, the real rate of growth of GDP may be estimated at 11 per cent. In constant price terms, per capita GDP rose by an estimated 7 per cent annually. The performance is far from unsatisfactory in aggregate terms. Yet, there were important differences in growth rate between the first and second parts of the decade. From 1959 to 1964, GDP rose by 16.1 per cent on an average annual basis, compared with 8.1 per cent from 1964 to 1968. (See Table 3.)

The high growth rate during the first part of the decade was due mainly to the explosive growth of the modern sector, dominated by the creation of an iron-mining complex in the north. Between 1959 and 1962, on the basis of unpublished figures, the largest increases in value added seem to be due to the construction phase of the MIFERMA iron mines. By 1964, the mines were in operation, and the contribution to value added was in the form of iron ore, although there was a nearly corresponding fall in building activity.

As Tables 3 and 4 make clear, transport and communications rose sharply between 1959 and 1964 and constituted the second important factor in the growth of GDP. In part, the growth of modern-sector GDP may be attributed to the

TABLE 3

Growth of GNP and GDP, 1959, 1964, and 1968[a]

Activity	1959 (billion CFAF)	Annual Growth Rates[b] (per cent)	1964 (billion CFAF)	Annual Growth Rates[c] (per cent)	1968 (billion CFAF)	Annual Growth Rates[d] (per cent)
GNP	15.7		29.3		39.0	
Net factor payments & remittances	+0.7		+5.3		+8.1	
Total (GDP)	16.4	16.1	34.6	8.1	47.1	12.5
GDP						
Traditional sector	11.3	4.8	14.2	7.2	18.8	5.8
Nonmonetary	6.9	4.2	8.4	3.0	10.6	4.9
Monetary	4.4	5.7	5.8	9.1	8.2	7.2
Modern sector	5.1	32.0	20.4	8.6	28.4	21.0
Mining & construction	0.7	6.4	8.7	17.4	16.5	41.0
Transport & communications	1.5	30.0	5.6	-0.7	5.4	15.5
Other	2.9	15.0	6.1	.1	6.4	9.0

a Totals do not add due to rounding.
b 1959=64.
c 1964=68.
d 1959=68.

Source: RIM, Ministère de la Planification et du Développement Rural, Comptes Economiques de la République Islamique de Mauritanie (1968).

TABLE 4

GDP, 1959, 1964, and 1968
(Million CFAF)

Activity	1959	1964	1968
GDP	16,383	34,580	47,144
Traditional Sector			
Nonmonetary			
Agriculture	1,565	1,650	1,670
Livestock	800	800	810
Dairying	4,400	5,775	7,900
Fishing	100	200	180
Total	6,865	8,425	10,560
Monetary			
Agriculture	520	925	1,380
Livestock	2,798	3,247	4,220
Dairying	400	600	700
Fishing	320	583	1,248
Handicrafts	328	400	613
Others	30	40	52
Total	4,396	5,795	8,213
Total traditional sector	11,261	14,220	18,773
Modern Sector			
Mining & construction	737	8,695	16,502
Transport & communications	1,493	5,595	5,445
Services	202	499	1,150
Public enterprises	-	213	1,236
Government salaries	2,690	5,358	4,038
Total modern sector	5,122	20,360	28,371

Source: RIM, Ministère de la Planification et du Développement Rural, Comptes Economiques de la République Islamique de Mauritanie (1968).

establishment of a relatively large, well-paid, expatriate and local population in the Port-Etienne and Zouerate area and to the rapid growth of the administrative capital at Nouakchott, with its growing class of Mauritanian and expatriate officials. The drop in administrative salaries after 1964 was due mainly to the reduction of French military expenditures. Public maintenance outlays were also curtailed during this period, and government personnel outlays did not rise sufficiently to offset this.

During the second half of the decade, from 1964 to 1969, the growth of GDP was about half that of the earlier period. This fall in the growth rate was due mainly to the leveling off in the rate of increase in iron-ore output as MIFERMA reached full production. There is little evidence of dramatic growth in the traditional nonmonetary livestock and agricultural sectors throughout the 1960's. Even the figures published, which show growth rates of from 4 per cent to 5 per cent annually, are not based on particularly reliable data for livestock and grain output. In a subsistence economy, with a slow rate of technological change, rises in output must have, at least approximately, a net growth in population of under 1 per cent annually. In the traditional monetary sector, there is evidence of higher rates of growth of output. In particular, the livestock sector, which produces both meat and milk, and the agricultural sector showed impressive rates of growth, due mainly to efforts to improve the health of herds during this period. In 1968 and 1969, a severe drought curtailed rural output and caused a reduction in the size of herds.

A word is in order on the relationship between GDP and GNP in Mauritania. GDP has been used for most of the sector analyses, as such breakdowns are not available for GNP. GNP figures are heavily influenced by the large modern-sector factor payments and private salary transfers related to the enclave foreign-owned mining industry and the large expatriate technical assistance population. These payments rose from almost nothing in 1959 to CFAF 5.3 billion in 1964 and to CFAF 8.1 billion in 1968.

RESOURCE AVAILABILITY AND USE

The availability of resources in recent years was in large part dependent on the output of the mining sector and the growth of services, as was indicated earlier. Important fluctuations

in domestic resource availability were, however, caused
principally by the large flow of investment funds into the mining
sector in 1962, which were matched by imports of goods and
related services from abroad.   Between 1962 and 1964, gross
capital formation fell from 67 per cent to 13 per cent of GDP. *
The effect of this large drop in capital formation on the economy
was relatively small, since most of the goods and services
used in the mining investment program were imported.

In effect, the wider economic impacts of this investment
were achieved mainly in the countries outside Mauritania that
supplied the capital and the bulk of the consumption goods required and where the bulk of the savings accruing in the modern
sector were repatriated.   The completion of the mining investments led to a drop in capital formation.   The advent of
a new period of heavy mining investment in Akjoujt is having
similar, although more muted, effects on gross investment,
GDP, and foreign trade.   Table 5 illustrates the growth of
investment in the three years 1959, 1964, and 1968.

Although investment tends to be volatile and temporary
in nature, due to the character of the mineral-extraction industry, the figures do show a substantial continuous rise in
national savings over the period.   National savings as a percentage of GNP rose from .2 per cent in 1959 to 5.4 per cent
in 1964 and 13 per cent in 1968.   The bulk of these savings
accrued in the private sector, but, in 1968, for the first time,
net public savings are recorded.   The savings figures reflect
the growth of per capita income in the modern and monetary
sectors.   In the subsistence economy, savings consist of increases in livestock herds and housing construction, which
are, by definition, equal to estimated investments.

The growth of modern-sector GDP benefited between 10
and 20 per cent of the population.   The rest of the population
also experienced improvements in their standard of living according to these figures, since rural output grew faster than
population did, at least in the monetary sector.   The severe
drought of 1968 and 1969, however, probably caused a significant, if temporary, drop in the standard of living of a good
part of the rural population.   Rising iron-ore exports were
principally responsible for the emergence of a surplus in the
balance of trade and services after 1964.   They were, of
course, balanced by the outflow of factor payments and expatriate salaries mentioned earlier.

---

*These figures are based on earlier national-accounts
estimates that are not entirely consistent with the official
figures available only for 1959, 1964, and 1968.

TABLE 5

Availability and Use of Resources, GDP and GNP, 1959, 1964, and 1968
(Billion CFAF)

Activity	1959	1964	1968
GDP			
GDP (at current market prices)	16.4	34.6	47.1
Balance of goods & services	+ 0.9	- 0.8	- 0.6
Total available domestic resources	17.3	33.8	46.5
Consumption	15.4	27.7	34.0
Investment	1.9	6.1	12.5
Domestic savings	1.0	6.9	13.1
GNP			
GDP (at current market prices)	16.4	34.6	47.1
Net factor payments & remittances	- 0.7	- 5.3	- 8.0
Total (GNP)	15.7	29.3	39.1
GDP (at current market prices)	16.4	34.6	47.1
Balance of goods & services	+ 0.9	- 0.8	- 0.6
Total available national resources	17.3	33.8	46.5
Consumption	15.4	27.7	34.0
Public	4.6	6.5	6.5
Private	10.8	21.2	27.5
Investments	1.9	6.1	12.5
Public	0.8	2.0	3.4
Private	1.1	4.1	9.1
National Savings	0.3	1.6	5.1
Public	n.a.	-0.9	1.0
Private	n.a.	2.5	4.1

Sources: RIM, Ministère de la Planification et du Développement Rural, Comptes Economiques de la République Islamique de Mauritanie (1968); and Provisional Comptes Economiques 1964 (Paris: Ministry of Cooperation, 1967).

INCOME AND EMPLOYMENT

The household account of the national accounts is notably inexact, because it is impossible to calculate consumption accurately in the absence of a family budget survey. It is, in effect, a residual account containing the unexplained errors of the other accounts. Some 60 per cent of household income is estimated to accrue to individual entrepreneurs. About half of this income is estimated to be on a nonmonetary barter basis, which adds a further measure of uncertainty to the estimates.

About 32 per cent of household income is in the form of wages and salaries, due almost entirely to the iron mines and public services, which contain large numbers of expatriates. The high savings of the household sector are believed to result mainly from the savings of the relatively highly paid expatriate group. In part, the magnitude of these savings may also be due to a lag in adaptation of consumption habits to the recent advent of relatively high money incomes in the modern sector.

In Chapter 2, an analysis was made of the relation between employment and income in the modern and traditional sectors. The conclusion was reached that, in the modern private sector, foreigners held one-third of the positions but earned some two-thirds of all wage and salary payments, a considerable proportion of which was transferred abroad. In the modern public sector, foreigners held 10 per cent of the positions and presumably earned a disproportionate share of wage and salary income as well. If account is taken of the estimate for 1968 that the traditional sector produced about 40 per cent of the GDP at market prices, it is evident that a relatively small proportion of the labor force in the modern sector (about 5 per cent) earned a disproportionate share of the national income.

The figures for 1968 show that progress has been made in the Mauritanization of employment in the private sector, although a large proportion of positions in the middle and, particularly, higher grades continue to be held by expatriates, while unemployment continues to be high among the unskilled in the modern-sector towns. The Unions des Industries et Entreprises ascribe this phenomena to the unavailability of Mauritanians with sufficient skills and motivation to perform at these levels. In order to speed up the entry of Mauritanians into the higher grades of employment, they recommend a more extended vocational training period, together with the introduction of a system of apprenticeship.

There also appears to be a serious problem of getting

workers to identify their interests with those of the firms employing them, a problem connected with the charge that the
government labor officials show hostility toward private enterprises in interpreting and applying labor laws. The low output
of qualified nationals and the competition for them from the
public administration make it unlikely that Mauritanization of
the top jobs can be greatly increased for some time. In general,
Europeans are paid as much as 100 per cent more in wages
than are Mauritanians in the same wage class, plus about 40
per cent more if fringe benefits and moving costs are included.
This would presumably provide an incentive for employers to
prefer local personnel, once they reach equal quality.

The extreme inequality of income distribution may be
seen from Table 6. In 1963, 10 per cent of wage earners
earned 56 per cent of private wages. By 1967, 14 per cent of
wage earners earned 65 per cent of all private wages. There
was some upward shift in the numbers entering higher wage
categories, as 72 per cent of the workers earned CFAF 20,000
or less in 1963, compared with 67 per cent in 1967.

The officially established minimum-wage scale, salaire
minimum inter-professional garanti (SMIG), remained un-
changed from 1961 to 1969, when it was increased by 15 per
cent. In January, 1965, all remaining professions were
brought under the salary scales, so that all workers under
salary or who received wages were included.* Nevertheless,
the rising cost of living and the demand for skilled workers
forced employers to raise average incomes by some 40 per
cent from 1962 to 1967. This has been the result partly of
the upgrading of jobs and personnel, particularly in mining
and services, and partly of the increased proportion of top
salaried personnel, most of whom are Europeans.** (See
Appendix Tables 4 and 5.) Social charges reportedly add
about 25 per cent to the wages cost of Mauritanian workers.

The SMIG minimum wage recognizes two economic zones.
In Zone I, covering the country's main urban and industrial
areas, the SMIG is CFAF 41.30 per hour for industry and
commerce and CFAF 37.30 per hour for agriculture. In Zone
II, covering the areas where traditional activities dominate,
the industry and commerce SMIG is CFAF 35.70 per hour and
the agriculture SMIG is CFAF 32.30 per hour.

---

*The government has its own salary scale for permanent
employees. A 5 per cent cost-of-living increase was granted
in 1965 to these employees.

**In both 1962 and 1968, some 70 per cent of the expatriates
were of African origin, and the rest were European.

TABLE 6

Monthly Wages in the Modern Private Sector, by Income Category, 1963, 1965, and 1967

Monthly Wage (CFAF)	1963				1965				1967			
	Wage Earners		Total Wages		Wage Earners		Total Wages		Wage Earners		Total Wages	
	Number	Per Cent of Total	Amount (thousand CFAF)	Per Cent of Total	Number	Per Cent of Total	Amount (thousand CFAF)	Per Cent of Total	Number	Per Cent of Total	Amount (thousand CFAF)	Per Cent of Total
Up to 5,000	213	2.6	533	0.2	130	1.7	325	0.1	--	--	--	--
5,001-- 7,500	1,227	15.2	7,669	3.0	283	3.7	1,769	0.6	843	9.7	5,058	1.4
7,501--10,000	1,314	16.2	11,497	4.5	1,849	24.0	16,179	5.2	1,660	19.1	14,525	4.2
10,001--15,000	1,927	23.8	24,087	9.4	2,069	26.8	25,862	8.3	2,177	25.1	27,213	7.8
15,001--20,000	1,105	13.7	19,337	7.5	881	11.4	15,417	5.0	1,114	12.8	19,495	5.6
20,001--30,000	831	10.3	20,450	8.0	760	9.8	18,740	6.0	860	9.9	21,156	6.1
30,001--50,000	421	5.2	16,605	6.5	482	6.2	18,470	5.9	545	6.3	20,923	6.0
50,001--75,000	226	2.8	13,642	5.3	290	3.8	17,325	5.6	243	2.8	15,188	4.4
75,001 and over	826	10.2	142,974	55.6	974	12.6	196,410	63.3	1,246	14.3	225,374	64.5
Total	8,090	100.0	256,794	100.0	7,718	100.0	310,497	100.0	8,688	100.0	348,932	100.0

Sources: RIM, Ministère de la Planification et du Développement Rural, Annuaire Statistique (Nouakchott, 1968); and RIM, Bulletin Statistique et Économique (1968).

It is of further interest to examine recent trends in employment in the modern sector. From 1962 to 1965, total
modern-sector employment fell from over 20,000 to an estimated 18,700. The main reason for this decline was the fall
in expatriate employment from 5,174 to 2,560, mainly in the
private sector, or from 39 per cent to 32 per cent of the
total. (See Appendix Table 6.) The completion of the construction phase of the iron mines, together with the gradual
Mauritanization of positions, particularly in the lower and
middle grades, were principally responsible. Public-sector
employment of expatriates also declined sharply (from 1,100
to 640) during this period, although public-sector employment
rose steadily in total.

In the private sector, total employment fell by some
3,000 workers through 1965, due mainly to the laying off of
some 5,000 workers following the completion of the iron-
mining complex and related railway. The bulk of these either
were reabsorbed into the traditional sector or continued to
seek employment on the fringes of the modern sector. This
decline in employment was only partially compensated for by
rises in mining operating personnel. In total, modern-sector
employment of Mauritanians stabilized at about 13,000 from
1962 to 1965. This compares with a total estimated modern-
sector employment of 4,800 in 1957.

Despite the creation of a government administrative apparatus and the coming into operation of a major industrial
apparatus with related service activities, the demand for
workers was stabilized after 1962, while great shifts occurred
in types of skills and educational backgrounds needed, particularly from construction to operating and maintenance personnel
in the mines. Public building activity also diminished, because
of the ending of construction of the major part of the new
capital. The slow growth of industrial processing is evident
from the breakdown of private-sector employment between
1957 and 1967 in Appendix Table 7. Even the service sector--
including banking, transport, and commerce--which experienced a threefold rise in value added between 1962 and 1964,
required apparently fewer personnel to maintain this output
by 1967.

From 1965 to 1968, modern-sector employment rose slowly
from some 18,700 to nearly 19,400. (See Table 7.) The
principal changes took place in commerce and other services,
where declines in employment were offset by rises in building
and construction employment, presumably partly in connection with the start of construction on the Akjoujt copper-mining

TABLE 7

Employment of Mauritanians and Non-Mauritanians in the Modern Sector, by Activity, 1965-68

Activity	November 30, 1965			November 30, 1966			November 30, 1967			November 30, 1968[a]		
	Mauritanian nationals	Non-Mauritanians	Total	Mauritanian nationals	Non-Mauritanians	Total	Mauritanian nationals	Non-Mauritanians	Total	Mauritanian nationals	Non-Mauritanians	Total
Public sector[b]	--	--	11,000	--	--	12,000	--	--	10,500	--	--	10,500
Private sector												
Agriculture & fishing	397	73	470	430	59	489	518	65	583	518	65	583
Mining & quarrying	2,619	1,262	3,881	2,825	1,250	4,075	2,928	1,250	4,178	2,978	1,211	4,189
Processing industry	148	109	257	164	116	280	228	185	413	258	215	473
Commerce & other services	1,116	559	1,675	1,063	550	1,613	1,118	481	1,599	1,118	481	1,599
Building & construction	983	452	1,435	1,436	395	1,831	1,540	502	2,042	1,540	502	2,042
Total private sector	5,263	2,455	7,718	5,918	2,370	8,288	6,332	2,483	8,815	6,412	2,474	8,886
Total salaried employment	--	--	18,718	--	--	20,288	--	--	19,315	--	--	19,386

[a] Preliminary.
[b] Estimated.

Source: RIM, Bulletin Statistique et Economique (1968).

48

complex.   Mauritanian employment increased by over 300 in
mining from 1965 through 1968, reflecting the continued
Mauritanization of employees at the MIFERMA mines.   The
biggest rise was in Mauritanians employed in building and
construction.

MINING

Iron Ore

The relatively high-grade iron-ore deposits in northern
Mauritania near Fort-Gouraud are being exploited by MIFERMA,
a company consisting of French, English, Italian, and German
shareholders. Total investments through 1966 were in excess
of $200 million; the bulk of the plant and equipment, including
large processing facilities and a railroad, were completed by
the end of 1963. The Mauritanian Government acquired a 5
per cent share in the enterprise when exploitation began in
1963.

The most important external source of finance was a 6.25
per cent, fifteen-year loan of CFAF 16.3 billion ($66 million)
from the IBRD granted in March, 1960, and guaranteed by
France and Mauritania. In addition, the company received a
CFAF 2.5 billion, 3 per cent, twenty-four-year Caisse Centrale
de Coopération Economique loan and a CFAF 5.25 billion loan
from the French Treasury in two parts, with terms of 5.6 per
cent for thirteen years and 6-6.5 per cent for twelve years,
respectively, partly guaranteed by the French Government. A
consortium of French banks also granted a medium-term re-
volving credit of CFAF 3.5 billion, rediscountable with the
Credit National of France. The guarantees of the two governments, as well as the concessional terms of a small part of the
financing, amounted to a subsidization of the project.

The MIFERMA project was originally regarded as the key to the future economic development of the country that would enable it to accelerate the pace of very slow progress that its otherwise limited resources made possible. It was to bring the age of industrialization to Mauritania, while providing budgetary surpluses that would make the country self-supporting, as well as able to finance an investment program. In fact, its influence on the economy in terms of income, employment, and technological change has been slight, while it has not lived up to expectations in providing revenues to the state budget.

MIFERMA has not been able to earn the profits originally projected because of a combination of rising costs and reduced international prices of iron ore. This situation exists even though operations started in 1963, a year earlier than originally anticipated. By 1965, actual output had exceeded the original projections for that date by 50 per cent. Output for 1966, which was supposed to reach 5.3 million tons, in fact rose to 7.2 million tons.

The rise in output was due to a considerable increase in proven ore reserves, [*] together with the tight financial position of the firm caused by the drop in prices and higher-than-anticipated operating costs (particularly of rail transportation of the ore), which made it desirable to spread fixed costs over a large output. Nevertheless, by the end of 1966, total cumulative payments to the government under the long-term tax scheme amounted to CFAF 4.7 billion, compared with the CFAF 5.7 billion originally projected. Without the rise in output, the shortfall to the budget from this source would have been considerably greater.

Even with these adjustments in total output, the future prospects for the company were not bright because of the likelihood of further decreases in iron-ore prices and increasing costs. Although there were times when overseas demand for ore appeared to be uncertain, the basic long-term limitation to increased sales was productive capacity. A considerable proportion of total output is bought usually at some discount from the regular price by steel mills, which own more than 50 per cent of MIFERMA shares.

The company revived the idea of exploiting the relatively rich F'Derik deposits, previously postponed because of the relatively tight financial situation and the increases in output

---

[*]According to one estimate, proven reserves amount to some 144 million tons, excluding extracted mixed ores of less than 60 per cent iron content.

achieved in other deposits. Investment for an additional capacity of some 1.5 million tons a year at F'Derik is estimated
to cost substantially less per ton than in the rest of the enterprise. The developing of the estimated 27 million tons of ore
deposits at F'Derik will require a further CFAF 5 billion
($20 million). In order to avoid the excessive financial burden
that the payment of the full import duty on machinery and equipment would have required, a new protocol was signed in 1966,
to expire in 1971, that essentially limited total taxes to 9 per
cent of the free-on-board (f. o. b.) value of exports of ore, assuming these exceeded 5.5 million tons. *

With the new protocol and the higher sales made possible
by the exploitation of the F'Derik deposits, total taxes for the
period 1966-75 are conservatively projected to increase from
an estimated CFAF 7.8 billion to CFAF 13.2 billion. The firm
plans to finance the entire investment from current cash generation and from medium-term suppliers' credits. The higher
taxes and higher interest payments on short-term borrowings
can be expected to depress profits temporarily; although,
later, the lower cost of producing high-quality ore at F'Derik
is expected to be of substantial benefit to the firm.

MIFERMA produces about 30 per cent of the GDP and
accounts for three-fourths of Mauritania's exports, based on
production of an estimated 83 million tons in 1969, with exports
valued at CFAF 17.5 billion. By 1970, MIFERMA's estimated
contribution to the GDP through output of ore and investment
will begin to decline slowly, while its contribution to government revenues and thus to the public development program will
be approximately stabilized. MIFERMA's contribution to the
budget and to development may well be higher when account is

---

*Under usual procedures, the over-all tariff burden on
machinery and equipment is 14.2 per cent on imports from
EEC countries and ranges from 19.9 per cent to 48.5 per
cent on imports from non-EEC countries granted the minimum
tariff; under the new arrangement, in fact, the import duties
due are to be debited to a special account, to be written off
against the 9 per cent export tax paid, contingent tax credits
built up by MIFERMA through the payment of earlier taxes,
and income taxes that would have to be paid in the event earnings were large enough. As in the past, payments made by
MIFERMA to the government of Mauritania are regarded as
advances against the 50 per cent of the profits that are to accrue to Mauritania, should the firm ever be in a position to
earn such profits.

taken of the fact that its employees constitute about one-fifth of modern-sector employment and, in view of their relatively high salary scales, probably a higher proportion of the income taxes and indirect taxes paid by people earning modern-sector incomes. On the other hand, precise calculation of a wider impact would have to take into account higher government outlays per capita for schools, infrastructure and other services in the modern sector including the MIFERMA area.

Plans call for an expansion of. output up to some 11 million tons by 1973, through use of a higher proportion of low-grade ores. The port of Cansado is being enlarged at a cost of CFAF 1.4 billion to handle the additional exports. For the longer term, there are prospects for mining up to 2 billion tons of 40 to 45 iron-content deposits some 30 km. north of the present mining site. Whether this exploitation will take place will depend on world prices and whether a concentration process can be developed that does not require large quantities of water. It would seem that substantial economies could be effected in prolonging the life of iron-ore deposits, since much of the investment in such basic infrastructure as ports, buildings, and a rail system are already in place.

Copper

The existence of copper deposits at Akjoujt, some 250 km. northeast of Nouakchott, has been known of since 1931. According to the most recent estimates by a Canadian firm, open-pit reserves consist of 7.7 million tons of oxide ores containing 2.52 per cent copper and 19.9 million tons of sulphide ores containing 1.76 per cent copper. There are indications of the existence of more sulphide ores underlying the open-pit deposits, which may have to be mined by underground methods if their exploitation proves to be feasible in the future.

Several concessions were granted for the exploitation of the Akjoujt deposits starting in 1951. Through 1965, all the concessionnaires had failed to solve the technical problem of concentrating the oxide ore, with its high carbonate content, or to reach satisfactory financial agreements among themselves. In November, 1966, the proposal of Anglo-American International--through a subsidiary, Charter Consolidated Ltd.--for exploiting the deposit with its new and still experimental Torco process was accepted by the Mauritanian Government.

Under the terms of a convention signed with the Mauritanian

Government, an operating company called the Société Minière
de Mauritanie (SOMIMA) was set up in Mauritania. The convention was ratified at the end of June, 1967, by the Mauritanian National Assembly. The total estimated investment
amounted to $59.8 million, which included $3.7 million to repay the Société des Mines de Cuivre de Mauritanie (MICUMA)
interest in the concession. Agreement on the final financial
arrangements was reached in 1968.

   The share-capital distribution was changed after the
participation of the International Finance Corporation (IFC)
in the venture; Charter gave up its majority, and other groups
agreed to a diminution in their shareholdings. Total share
capital is now $8 million, distributed as follows:

Charter Group	44.6%
Islamic Republic of Mauritania	22.0%
French Group	18.4%
IFC	15.0%

The shareholders further agreed to advance $15 million in
subordinated loans to the company on a pro rata basis to
their equity holdings. The balance of $36.8 million of re-
quired investment is to be obtained from an IFC unsecured
loan of $12.2 million, and IFC secured loan of $4.3 million,
a European Investment Bank (EIB) guaranteed loan of $11
million, and loans from such other banks as Credit Lyonnais
and the Banque Internationale de l'Afrique Occidentale (BIAO)
totaling $9.3 million.

   In the event additional funds are required during the phase
when production shifts from oxide to sulphide ores, Charter
and the shareholders other than the government and the IFC
have undertaken to provide them in the form of a subordinated
loan at a rate of interest in excess of 8 per cent. The IFC
will contribute $20 million of the total investment, and the
EIB, $11 million. By 1976, cumulative dividends distributed
are expected to exceed shareholders' equity. The agreement
with the IFC contains restrictions on the payments to shareholders in excess of repayments on IFC and EIB loans. According to the projections, dividends will not be paid on shares
until 1975, although shareholders' loans should be paid up by
this time, thus making the shares marketable.

   SOMIMA has to pay an export duty of U.S. 1 cent per pound
of copper contained in the exported concentrates sold when the
f.o.b. price in Nouakchott is less or equal to 40 cents per pound.
This rises to 1.25 cents for a price of more than 40 cents and

less or equal to 50 cents per pound. For a price above 50
cents, the export duty rises to 1.5 cents per pound.

The company is exempt from income taxes during a five-
year period beginning on the date of the first commercial ship-
ment of marketable concentrates. The company and enterprises working for its account are exempt from all customs
taxes and duties on all necessary imported merchandise,
materials, machinery, equipment, spare parts, and consum-
able goods. Although SOMIMA has, in fact, the right to transfer funds freely out of Mauritania, given the present effective
convertibility of the CFAF, the convention restricts the right
of Mauritania to impose foreign exchange controls in the future.

SOMIMA has agreed to construct and maintain the Nouak-
chott-Akjoujt road on a joint basis with the government. The
company was originally obliged to construct and maintain
necessary facilities at the wharf, but it now appears that financing will be obtained from FED for this purpose, with
SOMIMAs undertaking a larger share of the construction and
maintenance of the road than was originally anticipated. Further, it has undertaken to provide housing, water, medical,
and recreation facilities for its employees. It will also give
preference to qualified local labor and will train such labor.

The government's obligations to provide infrastructure
to support the venture will be partly financed by a loan of
CFAF 185 million from SOMIMA at 6.5 per cent interest, to
be repaid in five annual installments starting in 1976 and ending in 1982, according to the financial projections. From the
point of view of the government and of the economy, the primary impact of Akjoujt will be on the revenues of the state
either in the form of taxes or as the state's share in profits.

The financial projections of the enterprise are based on
an international price of 37.5 cents per pound for copper,
which is believed to be a conservative basis for estimating
returns. Given the initial income-tax exemption and write-
off provisions, the project will not produce revenues from
income tax until nine years after the start of construction in
1967. Significant returns from income taxes are not anticipated until 1980-81, when the state will receive an estimated
CFAF 800-900 million annually.

The venture is, nevertheless, calculated to be quite
profitable. The internal rate of return is estimated at 16.6
per cent annually. The yield will be significantly affected by
changes in the price of copper. For example, every 1-cent
increase in the price per pound of copper will increase sales
revenue $650,000 annually. Mauritania will not acquire free

financial resources for its budget at the same rate as dividends
are distributed, since it must repay from the first distribution
of income some $4.5 million that it is expected to borrow from
the Caisse Centrale for its share of the shareholders' contributions. FAC will reportedly make available a grant for the
balance of Mauritania's contribution. Moreover, Mauritania
must make repayments to SOMIMA on account of its borrowing for government-provided infrastructure.

   According to recent financial projections, it is unlikely
that distributions to shareholders in all forms will be sufficient
to enable Mauritania to repay these amounts fully before 1976.
On this basis, Mauritania's budget will receive no benefit from
shareholders' distributions until seven years after the start of
construction. Table 8 indicates the returns that Mauritania is
likely to receive from the copper project from 1970 to 1974.
In terms of resources to finance the second plan period (1970-
73), the copper project will yield virtually nothing. Through
the end of the exploitation period in mid-1988, Akjoujt will
yield an estimated total of CFAF 12 billion in export duties,
income taxes, and shareholders' distributions.

   In terms of employment, it is expected that jobs will be
provided for some 480 personnel, of whom ninety-six will be
Europeans. There will no doubt be further gains to national
income and employment from the service and complementary
activities that can be expected to come into existence when the
copper mine is in operation. Yet, the experience so far with
MIFERMA indicates that these indirect effects will be limited
in scope.

   The construction phase of Akjoujt should involve the temporary employment of a considerable number of relatively unskilled workers who, by and large, will not be able to find
permanent employment in the modern sector, as happened in
the case of the iron mines. The creation of a new town, with
its requirement for modern communications, education, and
social services, can also be expected to place a new burden
on the capital and current budgets of the state. The net financial gain to the budget, accordingly, may be less than projected above; and, in the initial years, the cost of Akjoujt to
the budget could even exceed the returns therefrom.

   The over-all economic impact of the Akjoujt project will
be something less than half that of the MIFERMA iron-ore
enterprise but will, nevertheless, be considerable in view of
the disproportionate share of mining in the GDP. The contribution of Akjoujt to the GDP, calculated on a gross value added
from construction, began during the second half of 1967, when

TABLE 8

Estimated Mauritanian Government Receipts
from Akjoujt, 1970-74 (calendar years)

Year	Export Duty (million CFAF)	Indirect Income[*] (million CFAF)
1970	64.5	51.5
1971	145.5	51.5
1972	156.3	51.5
1973	156.3	51.5
1974	156.3	51.5

[*]Estimated income from taxes on service and other
activities that will come about as a result of various demands
created by the existence of the mine.

Source: 1967 IBRD mission.

an estimated CFAF 750 million was added to the GDP. This
rose steadily through the main investment period which ended
in 1970, with an estimated contribution of CFAF 2.6 billion
to the GDP. During the exploitation period, the copper mine
is expected to contribute about 13 per cent to the GDP, depending on the sale of concentrated ore and the new investments undertaken.

Other Minerals

During the first three years of the first plan period, a
modest sum of some CFAF 210 million was provided and spent
for aerial and ground geophysical studies. As a result, interesting indications were found of chrome, beryl, and fluorite.
Further evidence was found of two gypsum deposits near
Nouakchott, totaling some 2 million tons. Together with known
deposits, there may be reserves of some 3 million tons of
gypsum of high quality. Export of this gypsum to nearby African countries may be possible from the expanded wharf facilities at Nouakchott.

Given the limited domestic market and the absence of
other inputs, the production of cement in Mauritania does not

appear to be feasible at present, particularly since sea transport costs from Rufisque are likely to be sharply reduced once
the wharf at Nouakchott is expanded. Mauritania also has
large, widely distributed and unexploited reserves of limestone.
By using these domestic limestone deposits in construction,
Mauritania could economize on the import of some 10,000 tons
of cement annually, particularly for smaller buildings in the
interior provinces. Cement costs CFAF 12,500 a ton to deliver
in Nouakchott and CFAF 50,000 a ton in Nema in the Eastern
Hodh.

Readily accessible phosphate deposits of some 4 million
tons exist, and it is probable that reserves are far greater.
Phosphate could be used for domestic agriculture in the river
basin, once production is based on a more advanced technology,
although competition from Senegal and Río de Oro must be
reckoned with.

Until 1955, salt output amounted to close to 10,000 tons
annually, mainly in the Trarza. Competition from sources
in Mali and Senegal caused output to drop to some 600 tons
annually. In the future, Akjoujt and the Port-Etienne fish-
processing industry will become major users of salt. In this
connection, the desalinization plant under construction at
Nouakchott may put Mauritania in a superior competitive position to supply this need.

Oil prospecting has been under way by several companies,
notably the French-owned Petrobar and the American-owned
Planet Oil Company. Planet proposed to spend CFAF 375
million over five years, including offshore prospecting. Esso
reportedly plans to apply for a permit involving an expenditure
of CFAF 160 million. All exploration so far has been in the
form of geological surveys.

FISHING

The waters bordering Mauritania's Atlantic coast near
Port-Etienne are quite rich in fish resources. The annual
yield from these waters is estimated to be from 200,000 to
300,000 tons of edible fish, with a value of up to CFAF 20
billion and the use of some 600 vessels of all kinds. In 1968,
only 16,400 tons of fish for drying were landed, mainly by a
Canary Islands fishing fleet based in Port-Etienne. In addition, there is a small local fleet, as well as a few Imaraguen
tribesmen, who fish from canoes along the coast, largely for

their own consumption. There are probably not more than
300 Mauritanian fishermen, and their total annual earnings
are estimated to be on the order of CFAF 25 million.

This fish is salted and dried for export to the Democratic
Republic of Congo, the People's Republic of Congo, Gabon,
and Ghana. Some 5,300 tons of frozen fish were sent by the
fishing industry of Port-Etienne to France, Italy, and Greece
in 1968. The bulk of the catch in waters near Mauritania is
exported directly to Europe in fresh or frozen form by an international fishing fleet. Fishing in the Senegal River is estimated
to yield some 15,000 tons of fish annually (value CFAF 500 million) by 500 full-time and 10,000 part-time fishermen, who
supplement their farm incomes in this way. Most of it is consumed by the riparian population of some 200,000 people, largely in fresh form.

Table 9 gives the breakdown in 1968 of production, consumption, and exports of fish in Mauritania. Mauritanian
domestic consumption of fish is about 12,300 tons, by some
340,000 people. The Moors eat virtually no fish. Prices of
fish vary widely. At the Senegal River, the price per kilo is
about CFAF 25 and, at Nouakchott, CFAF 60. Dried fish
sold by the Imaraguen yields between CFAF 20 and 30 per kilo
delivered. For drying at Port-Etienne a price of CFAF 40 is
paid.

The first four-year plan called for investments in Port-
Etienne that would establish discharge and processing facilities
for 50,000 tons of fresh fish annually. In fact, investments
made and in process of completion created by 1968 a theoretical
processing capacity of 300,000 tons of fresh fish annually, although the port could handle the discharge of only 50,000 tons.
These investments in port equipment, freezing and cold-storage
plants, vessels, and fishmeal and drying plants total some
CFAF 7 billion on the part of various foreign investors and the
Mauritanian Government. Public funds, including the Caisse
Centrale loans, account for CFAF 3.7 billion of this and private
investments about CFAF 3.4 billion. The private contribution
contains only 10 per cent of equity investment, with the balance
provided by loans from the Mauritanian Development Bank
(Banque Mauritanienne de Développement, BMD), the Caisse
Centrale, the Banque Dreyfuss, and suppliers' credits.[*]

The investment decisions already taken in the Port-Etienne
fishing industry resulted in a serious imbalance between port

[*]See R. Westebbe, Guidelines for a Four-Year Develop-
ment Program for Mauritania, "Report by 1967 IBRD Technical
Assistance Mission" (Washington, D.C.: IBRD, July, 1968),
Vol. I, paras. 184-91, and Vol. II, paras. 243-60.

TABLE 9

Fish Consumption and Exports, 1968

Item	Total Tonnage	Consumption for Households		Enterprises	Official Exports
		Self-Consumption	Commercial		
Senegal River	15,000	7,000	5,000	3,000	--
Nouakchott	150	20	130	--	--
Cap Timiris & others	800	70	130	600	--
Port-Etienne					
for drying	16,400	--	--	16,400	--
for freezing	5,260	--	--	--	5,260
Total	37,610	7,090	5,260	20,000	5,260
Lobsters	36	--	1	--	35
Other	16	--	1	--	15
Salted & Dried Fish	6,700	--	375	--	6,375

Source: République Islamique de Mauritanie, Ministère de la Planification et du Développement Rural, Comptes Economiques de la République Islamique de Mauritanie (1968).

capacity and the capacity of the processing industries. Inadequate consideration was given to such elementary factors as the supply of fish in Mauritanian waters, the economic incentives for fishermen to use the processing facilities instead of shipping direct to Europe, and, finally, a rational appraisal of the market for Mauritanian processed fish in Europe, particularly France. In addition, there are serious grounds for questioning the huge amounts of public capital that have been invested directly in Port-Etienne or indirectly in the form of loans to private interests for the establishment of an industry based on such inadequate planning.

The processing industries already in existence were operating below capacity, a situation that will become more critical as new capacity is being completed. In fish drying and salting, two firms processed some 15,000 tons of fresh fish annually, yielding 5,000 tons of exportable product. Their theoretical capacity is 30,000 tons of fresh fish annually. An additional capacity of 30,000 tons came into existence as a Spanish firm completed its investment.

The cold-storage industries treated only 2,200 tons of fish in 1966, although capacity is some 22,000 tons. Capacity increased by 15,000 tons with the completion of a new freezing plant. The fishmeal industry is in the course of being established. It will have a theoretical annual capacity of some 210,000 tons of fish input on a single-shift basis, with a potential output of 40,000 tons of fishmeal. The canning industry is part of the Spanish complex and has a capacity to can 7,000 tons of fish annually.

In order to supply Port-Etienne with fish, a foreign group connected with the cold-storage industry placed an order abroad for fourteen large vessels, which should be able to land 24,000 tons of fresh fish annually. The first four vessels delivered did not yield satisfactory results. In the absence of an adequate Mauritanian fishing fleet, charter parties were made with French, Panamanian and Greek fishing vessels that fish in Mauritanian waters to supply fish to the Port-Etienne facilities. The fish were to retain the nationality of the vessels delivering them, and the foreign fishermen would remain responsible for the export and sale of the processed fish. A duty of CFAF 3 per kilo was levied for fish not landed. The duty was payable to the mixed (public and private) company making the contract. On the basis of evidence available, it appears that not more than half of the tonnage anticipated will be landed at Port-Etienne. Accordingly, the balance not landed will presumably be subject to the penalty.

In 1968, a financial crisis developed due to operating losses, which caused the Mauritanian Government as guarantor to enter into negotiations with the French and Dutch suppliers of the fishing vessels. Arrangements were sought for further FAC credits to enable the French suppliers to be paid, and some of the vessels have been leased for use elsewhere. The government's Fishing Service was moved to Port-Etienne, where it will come under the direct authority of the Office of the President, with a view to bringing about necessary reforms. A number of management changes have already taken place in the processing industry in order to put them on a sounder business basis. In 1970, a one-year renewable agreement was made with Japan giving permission to fish in Mauritanian waters upon payment of a tax and a guarantee to purchase shore-processed fish.

A number of fundamental problems will continue to plague the Port-Etienne fishing industry. First, under the provisions of the Merchant Marine and Fisheries Code of 1962, Mauritanian territorial waters were extended to six miles, while fishing in the adjacent six miles was subjected to regulation. Under the terms of a more recent act, on January 21, 1967, Mauritanian territorial waters were further extended to twelve miles, based on a straight line running from Cap Blanc to Cap Timiris. This extension brings under Mauritanian control the bulk of the fishing grounds off Port-Etienne. Other maritime fishing nations have not recognized this unilateral extension of Mauritania's territorial waters, although this does not mean that a confrontation is inevitable. Mauritania has a small police fleet that has improved its capacity for enforcing its authority in this area.

Second, the stock of exploitable marine resources appears to be diminishing because of overfishing by the large international fleet. Yields have fallen significantly in recent years, and yet no study is available of the area that could lead to a national policy for limiting future catches.

Third, the potential market for Mauritanian processed fish is not known. At present, the catch from Mauritanian waters is marketed directly in Europe by a well-established and experienced fleet. They will not readily yield their position to a Mauritanian fleet, nor has any effective way been found to induce them to use the excess processing capacity at Port-Etienne instead of the facilities in European ports. All this brings into question plans for establishing a competitive Mauritanian fleet and training large numbers of seamen, except possibly over the long run. It is estimated that it will

take some ten years to train in the Mamadou Touré School at
Port-Etienne the 1,200 seamen required to man a Mauritanian
fleet.

6

LIVESTOCK

During the first four-year plan, investments of some CFAF 600 million were made in the livestock sector, out of a projected CFAF 1,035 million for the full four years. During the first three years of the second plan, a considerable effort was made to provide sanitary protection for the herds. This consisted of an investment of CFAF 74 million for twenty new immunization parks, in addition to seventy-nine existing parks and the establishment of an immunization center. Unfortunately, the equipment provided was of limited effectiveness because inadequate transport was made available to the veterinarian service. Vehicles in service deteriorated rapidly because of lack of maintenance. The sanitation problem is particularly acute, as the herders suffer severe losses because of disease. In the absence of adequate statistics, the magnitude of such losses are difficult to estimate; however, the Mauritanian Livestock Service estimates that pneumonia alone caused losses in 1966 in excess of CFAF 100 million, despite the 700,000 vaccinations given that year.

A major limitation on livestock production is lack of sufficient water to enable the vast pastures to be exploited. The digging of wells at selected points in the pastures would enable the herds to survive the six-month dry season. It is estimated that one well could serve a sufficiently large area to water and pasture 10,000 animals. Only modest progress was made in this field during the first plan period. Some CFAF 375 million was spent for twenty wells and the establishment of one maintenance team. In general, well maintenance is badly deficient, for the communities lack financial resources and nothing is provided from the state budget.

It is estimated that 160,000 heads of families earned an average of CFAF 100,000 from livestock herding. Table 10 shows the estimated size of livestock herds according to official sources. The figures clearly indicate the sharp fall in livestock herds in 1969, the second year of the drought. In 1967, some 31,000 tons of meat were consumed domestically. Of this, 17,000 tons were eaten by the herders themselves, 1,700 tons were sold in rural areas, and 4,300 tons were used in urban centers. Consumption of meat varies greatly within the country. It is lowest among the farmers along the Senegal River and highest among the nomads and town dwellers. (See Table 11.)

Most livestock produced is exported on the hoof to Dakar and is not recorded in official statistics. In 1968, some 52,000 cattle were estimated to have been exported unofficially, and 18,000 were officially recorded, out of a total of 190,000 head produced. Similarly, some 330,000 goats and sheep were estimated to have been exported unofficially, and 270,000 were officially recorded in 1968.[1] The herds produced an estimated 10 per cent rate of return in 1968. (See Appendix Table 8 for a breakdown of the value of livestock and milk products consumed locally and exported.)

Milk is by far the most important output of the livestock sector for the noncommercialized nomadic economy. As Table 4 shows, dairying in 1968 produced CFAF 7.9 billion of the estimated GDP for the nonmonetary traditional sector, and meat only CFAF 810 million. In the monetary traditional sector, the situation is reversed; meat production accounted for CFAF 4.2 billion of the GDP, and milk CFAF 700 million. (See also Appendix Table 9.) In 1959, milk output was estimated at 509 million liters and, in 1968, 580 million liters, about three-fourths of which is cow's milk. The 580 liters of milk were consumed as follows: 360 liters by the nomads, 65 liters by sedentary households, and 35 liters by the urban population; 30 liters were turned into butter and 150 liters were used in feeding animals.[2] For the nomad, milk is, in fact, the principal source of food.

A beginning was made in the processing of meat by the decision to construct an abattoir and refrigeration plant at Kaedi with limited cold-storage facilities. The total cost is estimated at CFAF 200 million, of which CFAF 178 million

TABLE 10

Size of Livestock Herds, by Category, 1959-69
(Thousand Head)

Herd	1959	1964	1967	1968	1969
Cattle	1,250	2,000	2,275	2,300	2,000
Sheep & goats	8,000	4,600	6,550	6,700	5,800
Camels	500	500	710	720	720
Asses	200	250	280	300	300

Source: République Islamique de Mauritanie (RIM),
Ministère de la Planification et du Développement Rural,
Comptes Economiques de la République Islamique de Mauritanie
(1968).

TABLE 11

Estimated Meat Consumption, 1968

Population Grouping	Amount of Population	Annual Per Capita Consumption (in kg.)	Tons
Rural sedentary	170	10	1,700
Nomad	820	30	24,600
Urban	150	30	4,500
Total	1,140		30,800

was provided by FAC and the rest by the state equipment budget. The plant came into operation, behind schedule, in January, 1968, with an annual capacity of 2, 500 tons of meat. Three-quarters of the output is destined for export, with the rest going to such urban centers as Nouakchott, Port-Etienne, and Atar. Since the European market was closed for health reasons, the hope was to ship the meat by air to the Canary Islands. A trial order was obtained to ship 1, 000 tons of meat to the Canaries through a combination of airlift to Nouakchott and thence by boat. This attempt was not successful.

Assuming no return freight, meat exported by air will yield little or no profits at the 2, 500-ton production level, and losses will be incurred at output levels below 1, 500 tons annually. Losses may, therefore, be anticipated in the initial period. There is, further, the problem of inadequate supply of good-quality meat. No solutions have been found to the problems of collecting and fattening the animals, although a study was made, financed by FAC, of a collecting ranch.

The abattoir at Kaedi is run by a Mauritanian veterinarian, and the marketing of the meat is by a mixed French-Mauritanian company, in which the government has a minority share. A small abattoir has also been established at Nouakchott. A proposal exists for a refrigerator-abattoir complex at Kiffa with Yugoslav financing. In the absence of any convincing study or local experience to justify this project, serious doubts exist as to its economic feasibility.

A tannery was established in 1967 at Kaedi with private French and Mauritanian capital and a loan from the BMD. Some CFAF 90 million has been invested in a plant with a capacity of 30 tons of hides a month, which can readily be raised to 60 tons a month. The success of this venture depends on an adequate supply of high-quality hides from the new abattoir at Kaedi. Apparently, hides have been bought from as far away as Mali in the meantime, since the abattoir has produced too few.

AGRICULTURE

Agricultural developments may be considered in two main categories. First, and most important, is the traditional cultivation of millet-sorghum, either in the flood plain of the Senegal River of by the dry-farming method. Second are the attempts made to change production methods and productivity through capital-intensive hydroagricultural works. Under the first category, yields in the flood plain of the Senegal River vary between 250 and 750 kg. per hectare, with a national average of 400 kg.

Nothing has been done to raise these yields, except on an experimental basis. These experiments show that average increases in yields of some 200 kg. per hectare are relatively easy to obtain, generally through the use of light plowing (animal-drawn), early sowing, and the use of parasite-free seed. Far more spectacular results have been obtained with deep plowing, fertilizers, and higher-yielding seed, but the general applicability of these results has not yet been established. The partial modernization of farming through the use of animal-drawn plows will enable presently unused land to be brought under cultivation.

The construction of a number of rural dams to retain seasonal flood waters for millet and sorghum cultivation in the interior of the country has been encouraged by the government partly for political reasons and with FED financing. Unfortunately, the output of the inundated land is not sufficient to justify the cost of the dams, and overgrazing takes place near the dam sites because of the seasonal concentration of population and herds. An example of this are the dams of the east, constructed under the first four-year plan, which cost CFAF 350 million and which yield little or no return on the investment. Some 400 such dams have been constructed; they permit the seasonal inundation of about 6,000 hectares of land.

Yields of some 300 kg. per hectare are obtained in dry farming. They can be raised to 400 kg. per hectare with early sowing and improved methods of cultivation. Yields can exceed 600 kg. per hectare through the use of fertilizer; in selected experimental plots, far higher yields have been obtained.

A program of expanding the area under cultivation through use of animal-drawn plows has been under way for some time in Nema, in the Hodh Oriental. The plows and animals are financed by BMD loans to some thirty-eight farmers' associations, involving 670 farmers. The program has enabled the farmers to increase their output greatly and led initially to the increasing replacement of imported millet from neighboring Mali.

The plow scheme in Nema was a great success from a production point of view. The local governor recognized the problem that a large increase in production would create for a market with little current absorptive capacity. Accordingly,

the local government guaranteed a fixed purchase price, with
the expectation that farmers would store the millet until such
time as prices rose in the nonharvest season. In this way,
the scheme could operate with minimum public financing and
would rely on private producers to carry the bulk of the stock.

The devaluation of Mali's currency led to a flood of cheap
millet inputs from that country. Together with the sharp rise
in local output and the absence of any links with a national
storage-distribution and price-support scheme, the Nema ex-
periment collapsed. Farmers could not sell their millet at
remunerative prices and could not honor their debts for the
plowing equipment. This experience has led some analysts to
conclude that domestic demand will not support a great increase
in millet output and that, therefore, attention should be given
to capital-intensive irrigation works to produce rice and sugar,
for which demand is unsatisfied. Mauritania imports some
12, 000 tons of rice annually; output is about 700 tons.

Although irrigation has not produced satisfactory results,
the above proposition ignores the reality that, for some time,
millet and sorghum will be the main product of the Senegal
River farmers. Since this is virtually all they produce, they
have a comparative advantage over other areas. Even Senegal
advocated that farmers raise millet in that country's last
development plan, a fact that may augur well for Mauritanian
producers, who face no effective import barriers in Senegal.
In 1967, some 3,700 tons of millet and sorghum were exported
to Senegal, and 18,350 tons were shipped to destinations within
Mauritania. [3]

There is a good deal of dispute about how much is produced
in traditional agriculture. Official estimates for millet production for 1959 vary from 49,000 to 60,000 tons. Probable
consumption per capita indicates that as much as 80,000 tons
might have been produced. [4] Table 12 shows estimates of per
capita annual requirements for millet of Mauritania's main
population groupings. Output in a typical year thus probably
approximates 100,000 tons, although, in the 1968 drought year,
production reportedly fell to 47,000 tons, necessitating large-
scale imports of grain from abroad. In any given year,
Mauritania may also import and export millet from neighboring
Mali and Senegal.

The relatively isolated local production and consumption
markets of the country lead to surpluses of millet in one area
and deficits in another. This causes considerable differences
in prices between regions. Further, during the course of a
year, in any region, great variations in prices normally occur.

TABLE 12

Theoretical Requirements for Millet,
1959, 1964, and 1969[*]

Population Grouping	Annual Per Capita Consumption (in kg.)	Theoretical Consumption		
		1959	1964	1969
Nomad	75	54,800	60,000	61,500
Rural sedentary	140	21,000	22,500	23,800
Urban	95	5,700	9,500	14,200
Total	88 (average)	81,500	92,000	99,500

[*]These figures are close to the results shown by an empirical study for 1967, except for urban consumption, which is estimated at only 9,000 tons. See RIM, Les Exchanges Commerciaux en Mauritanie, "Report by SEDES, Paris" (Nouakchott, November, 1968), Vol. II.

Source: RIM, Ministère de la Planification et du Développement Rural, Comptes Economiques de la République Islamique de Mauritanie (1968).

Prices may be as low as CFAF 10 per kilo at harvest and may rise to CFAF 40 per kilo within three or four months. Stocks are held by merchants, who, during times of scarcity, sell at prohibitive prices and lend at exorbitant interest rates. The farmer must often go into debt in order to obtain enough food, clothing, and supplies to function, and he may not recover enough to extricate himself at harvest, when prices are at their lowest. The report of the 1967 IBRD technical assistance mission (Vol. II, Part I) suggested that an experimental system of precooperatives, improved inputs, animal-drawn plows, and extension services be introduced. This would be coupled with the establishment of local storage facilities and improvements in transport to link up the isolated markets better.

In the 1970-73 development plan, the government proposed a serious inquiry into establishing millet production objectives. A two-year household budget and survey of rural production

was started in 1970. [5] The object is to determine ways of
stabilizing prices and improving distribution.   Recognition is
given to the early needs for storage facilities in order to reduce, at least partially, the adverse impacts of speculation.
The Société Nationale Import-Export (SONIMEX), to be discussed in Chapter 7, is to take primary responsibility for
dealing with transport and storage facilities, as recommended
by the 1967 IBRD mission.

The prospects for bringing about a noticeable increase in
the well-being of the sedentary farmers may thus not be doomed
by the Nema experience.   It appears that there is substantial
suppressed demand for millet due to wide price fluctuations
within the year, and there are unexploited opportunities for
linking markets and making supplies available where they are
wanted.   Finally, the continuous availability of millet at stable
prices might induce a change in the consumption habits of those
nomads who come in contact with millet production and storage
centers.   The consumption patterns cited earlier indicate that
the diet of the nomad could be made more varied, if not improved, in nutritional value.

The hydroagricultural works so far undertaken in Mauritania
must be regarded as largely still in the experimental stage.
They consist of a number of pilot projects, such as at Boghé,
Dar El Barka, Keur Macene, and Lac R'Kiz, designed to show
how rice and other food crops could be produced on a profitable
basis through irrigation based at least in part on the pumping
of water.   These projects involve the construction of dikes and
the installation of fairly elaborate water-control equipment. [6]

These works have yet to produce results that can serve as
a satisfactory guide for further large-scale investments.   Aside
from serious errors in planning and execution, the experimental
plots have, in general, involved excessive capital costs in relation to the value of the crops that can be produced.   In some
cases, further studies are needed.   In the case of Boghé, more
knowledge is needed of the land-tenure system and the implications that this will have for further extensions of the area to be
improved.   The cost levels on the twenty-five-hectare experimental plot are too high to justify completion of the entire
proposed project.   Specifically, the problem that must be re-
solved in the near future is to produce two profitable crops,
rice and sorghum, with only supplementary irrigation by
pumping.

There is some prospect that it may ultimately be feasible
to develop a further 3,500 hectares in the lower Boghé plain
for growing rice by controlled submersion with supplementary

pumping. In addition, some 32,500 hectares could be developed in the region of the Gorgol River, of which 2,500 would be for sugar cane, through the construction of a reservoir dam at Foum El Gleita and a smaller dam at the north of the Gorgol River at the Senegal River. The scheme could lead to substantial increases in rice and sorghum output, as well as improved pasture for grazing, although it will require considerable preparation. Ultimately, Mauritania could also become self-sufficient in sugar, since the scheme envisages the construction of processing facilities for sugar cane that would be grown under irrigation below the dam. Some eight years would be required to complete the entire project, at an estimated cost of some CFAF 800 million.

The Chinese People's Republic has a 4,000-hectare rice project in the delta near Rosso. Yields approximate 1.5-2.0 tons per hectare, compared with an average of 0.8 per hectare obtained elsewhere. Chinese technicians and management are doing the entire project under a loan given to the government. Plans call for 6,000 tons of rice output by the end of the plan period. The project will not be economically viable, however, unless a way is found to produce two crops a year.

OTHER PRODUCTS

Little headway has been made in changing the production and marketing of dates. Experiments under way with date palms on a plantation basis in Konkossa have yielded limited results from the point of view of both quality and financial returns. The palm plantations of the Adrar have also made little progress because of disease; however, a program is under way to combat parasites. Meanwhile, a factory to prepare dates has been constructed in Atar with official French aid. Date production has been declining since 1959 because of generally drier conditions and the reduction in grand water levels in the Adrar as a result of pumping. Output is now estimated at some 12,000 tons annually, most of which is consumed domestically.

Most of the date-palm trees are owned by people whose primary occupation is livestock-raising. They spend little time in cultivating the trees and usually rent them for a season to others who consume and sell part of the crop locally. The returns on heavy investments in date-palm plantations with long lead times have not been sufficiently promising to cause

present owners or new entrepreneurs to want to improve
productivity. Present government efforts to improve processing and distribution and to control disease often seem like
the most prudent way to upgrade the industry. In addition, a
census is being taken under the 1970-73 plan of all palm
growers, and a study is being made of the market for dates,
both domestic and international.

Crops such as cotton and tobacco, which can be technically
produced in Mauritania, have not been cultivated because the
entire market would be outside the country, where wide price
fluctuations and generally low returns in relation to costs in-
hibit farmers. Vegetables are cultivated in a number of areas,
of which the most important is Atar, where they are grown on
the irrigated areas under the date-palm trees. Output is four
tons a month, whereas capacity is estimated at some ten tons.
The main problem is to persuade MIFERMA to purchase local
produce instead of importing from abroad. In this connection,
consideration will have to be given to questions of quality,
variety, and packing, as well as to MIFERMA procurement
policy.

Mauritanian gum production, the country's most venerable
export, reportedly doubled to 5,000 tons between 1959 and 1969.
It is gathered by individuals enjoying the right of exploitation
in a zone 50-100 km. wide between Mederdra to the south of
Nema. Destructive cutting practices threaten future yields,
and the Forestry Service lacks the resources to exercise
effective control. Some 1,500 tons of gum arabic are exported
annually through Dakar, where both marketing and processing
still exist. Some gum is consumed locally, and an important
part goes in unprocessed form to Mali without payment of
Mauritanian taxes. [7]

NOTES

1. République Islamique de Mauritanie (RIM), Ministère
de la Planification et du Développement Rural, Comptes
Economiques de la République Islamique de Mauritanie (1968).

2. Ibid.

3. See RIM, Les Exchanges Commerciaux en Mauritanie,
"Report by SEDES, Paris" (Nouakchott, November, 1968),
Vol. II.

4. See J. L. Boutillier et al. , La Moyenne Vallée du Sénégal, "Publication of the French Senegalese and Mauritanian Republics" (1962), pp. 173-92, for a detailed analysis of consumption standards in the valley by season and castes.

5. RIM, Deuxième Plan de Développement Economique et Social, 1970-1973 (Nouakchott, 1970), p. 14.

6. See R. Westebbe, Guidelines for a Four-Year Development Program for Mauritania, "Report by 1967 IBRD Technical Assistance Mission" (Washington, D.C.: IBRD, July, 1968), Vol. II, Part I, chap. ii.

7. See Les Exchanges Commerciaux en Mauritanie, Vol. I, pp. 132-36.

TRANSPORT

Government planning with respect to transport is dominated by three main policy considerations. First is the desire
to reduce dependence on Senegal for imported goods. Hence,
the creation of the wharf at Nouakchott and the construction of
a modern road from Nouakchott to Rosso, which is to link up
with the south and the west, replacing circuits dependent on
Dakar. Second is the goal of unifying the country by linking
the widely separated regions. Because of the vast distances
and dispersed population, major road works are difficult to
justify on economic grounds. Both air and river transport
assume special importance as a result. Third, transport
policy aims at contributing to the development of southern and
southeastern areas containing some 80 per cent of the population.

Mauritania's transport system serves three distinctly
different regions: the northern region to the north of the Port-
Etienne-Atar line, including the iron mines of MIFERMA at
Fort-Gouraud; the central region, including the capital
Nouakchott, and Akjoujt, the site of the copper-ore develop-
ment; and the southern and southwestern regions to the north
and east of the Senegal River, including the town of Rosso,
Boghé, Kaedi, Kiffa, and Nema.

The three regions are linked together by national highways
1 and 2, which form an L-shaped trunk route over 2,200 km.
from Fort-Gouraud in the north, via Nouakchott and Rosso in

the south, to Nema in the southeast. Most of this route is still in the state of a Sahara track, and, in the south, it is impassable during the rainy season; an all-weather road between Nouakchott and Rosso is under construction with an International Development Association (IDA)-EIB credit.

At present, there are only six km. of asphalt road connecting Nouakchott and the wharf. Of the rest, almost 4,000 km. of secondary tracks consist of branches from the main trunk routes connecting towns of lesser importance in the interior. There are no feeder roads in the ordinary sense of the term. The Kaedi-Kiffa road, financed with a CFAF 387 million FED credit, has been completed; but, because of poor planning and construction, most of the bridges have collapsed, and much of the work will have to be redone.

Road maintenance has been a serious deficiency. The policy of budgetary austerity limited funds available for roads. In 1968, a road-maintenance fund was established, to which the IDA contributed $3 million. A French firm was engaged to staff a housing center to train and direct a Mauritanian road-maintenance staff. Also, the size of the vehicle fleet is not accurately known. Estimates, which are believed to be inflated, indicate that, in 1968, there were some 9,500 vehicles in the country, of which 60 per cent were trucks, pick-ups, and buses. (See Appendix Table 23.) About 50 per cent of the registered trucks have a capacity of less than one ton. The 675-km. railway from Port-Etienne to Fort-Gouraud serves mainly to export iron ore, but it also carries general supplies.

The only proper port in Mauritania is Port-Etienne, which handled about 8 million tons of iron-ore exports; the commercial section of the port handled about 75,000 tons in 1969, mostly equipment, general supplies, and petroleum products. The port also serves the growing fishing industry. In Nouakchott, a wharf, financed by FED, was opened to traffic in June, 1966, and handles about 55,000 tons annually, largely rice and cement. Exports of copper ore began in late 1970. Imports at Nouakchott pay lighterage and high maritime surcharges. The wharf can compete with Dakar, for its high charges are offset by the costs of road transport from Dakar to many parts of Mauritania.

In the south, river navigation on the Senegal is the predominant mode of transport. Mauritania has three river ports: Rosso, Boghé, and Kaedi. Apart from light river craft, all commercial river transport is operated by a Senegalese company. Financing was requested but not obtained from

FED and one African development bank for the project of improving navigation on the Senegal River by removing certain obstacles.

In view of the vast distances and dispersed population, air transport has a large role to play, and Mauritania's aviation infrastructure is relatively well developed. It has twenty-two landing fields, but only Port-Etienne can receive transcontinental jet aircraft. The national airline operates five overage aircraft. It is reported to be running at a substantial annual deficit. A study of the line is under way, with the object of eventually introducing reforms.

FED has approved a grant of CFAF 220 million for extending and improving the Nouakchott airport, since nothing more sophisticated than a DC-6 could use this airport. Since Air Afrique is replacing their DC-6's with more modern equipment, it would have had to eliminate Nouakchott from its schedule unless the runways were improved.

The air fleet also possesses one Russian jetprop plane, which was given on very favorable terms, mainly to carry the President on his foreign travels. This aircraft, with its Russian maintenance and flight crews, was turned over to the national airline to be used on commercial flights. Unfortunately, its operating costs are reportedly so high that the airline loses more money by flying it than by keeping it grounded.

Total public investments for transport during the first four-year plan may amount to about CFAF 2.5 billion, excluding MIFERMA and the Nouakchott-Rosso road. By the end of this plan, major port investments were completed, and the air infrastructure was, by and large, sufficient to handle expected traffic. Investments for the reversal of trade flows will be completed well behind schedule, during the second plan with the construction of the Nouakchott-Rosso road.

By the end of the first plan, little progress was made toward improvements of the transport infrastructure in the south, an area of high priority in view of its dense population concentration and the importance of improved road connections for the livestock and agricultural sectors. A number of preparatory surveys and studies have been completed. For the future, the government would like to construct an all-weather road from Nouakchott to Nema in order to reduce the dependence of Nema on neighboring Mali. This road would, however, be quite costly and difficult to justify on economic grounds.

The policy of unifying the country around the capital at Nouakchott as a transport hub is questionable from an economic point of view. Admittedly, the political and social unification of the country can hardly succeed as long as large groups of inhabitants in the east and the south are more closely tied to Mali and Senegal economically than to Mauritania. Nouakchott has distinct limitations from a transportation point of view. It has no natural economic hinterland, with the exception of the copper mines. It is not the logical place to serve as a point of entry for consumer goods for the far north, the south, and the east; Port-Etienne, for example, is a far superior natural port. Recognition is given to the desirability of giving consumers the cost advantages of natural locations in the new plan, which suggests that the east could most economically be supplied with rice from Mali instead of through Nouakchott.*

ONTP

In 1964, a public organization was chartered under the name Office National des Transports Publics (ONTP) as the monopoly organization for bringing all road transport under public control. The ONTP was charged with centralizing the demand for road transport and allocating it between registered road-transport enterprises. The agency controlled entry into the industry through new-vehicle licensing and determined the share of individual transporters of the total traffic.

The ONTP fixed rates by region and commodity. It charged 5 per cent of freight income to cover its administrative expenses, to subsidize transport in specific regions, and to make a small contribution to road-maintenance expenditures through the state budget. The agency also transported for its own account and paid the same 5 per cent surcharge as commercial transport did. Consumption was subsidized in certain regions by the setting of artificially low rates.

In 1966, the ONTP had a total budget of CFAF 43 million, of which some CFAF 33 million was used for personnel, supplies, and buildings; CFAF 4 million for subsidies; and CFAF 5 million as a contribution to road maintenance. In 1965, 1966, and 1967, the ONTP gave a CFAF 4 million subsidy to transporters carrying oil and rice. The agency did not know the exact quantities transported, nor did it appear to have any policy with respect to the retail price of these commodities at their final point of consumption. State policy with respect

---

*République Islamique de Mauritanie, Deuxième Plan de Développement Economique et Social, 1970-1973 (Nouakchott, 1970), p. 84.

to supplying basic consumer goods will be discussed more
fully below.

In general, the system of central control of transport
operated to eliminate competition between transporters; there
are indications that rates were generous in relation to costs.
Such a system tended to preserve inefficient operators and to
raise the cost of transport to the economy as a whole, even
though rates were lower in some cases than those that pre-
vailed in the former era of private monopoly of transport.
The system was costly to administer, led to the undercutting
of rates in the interior, decontrolled shipments by those who
evaded the regulations, and cannot be said to have produced
high-quality transport services. Following the IBRD mission's
report, the ONTP was abolished early in 1968, and a new
system of maximum rates was introduced under the supervision of the Ministry of Transport. A road fund was set up
to subsidize transportation to the interior and to obtain its
resources from a gasoline tax.

SONIMEX

The function of SONIMEX is closely related to that of the
ONTP. This agency was set up in July, 1966, as a state
monopoly for the import and wholesale distribution of such
basic commodities as sugar, tea, rice, and cement. Originally, it was contemplated that the state would subscribe to
51 per cent of the CFAF 150 million capital of SONIMEX and
that private interests would absorb the rest. After an exten-
sive period of persuasion, private shareholders, mainly
several big firms, put up some 40 per cent of the total capital.
This reluctance to participate may be ascribed to several
factors, such as the knowledge that control would be in the
hands of the state, with limited opportunity for profit; the
refusal of the state to give shareholders any preference or
concessional price in allocating supplies to be distributed to
retailers; and the individualistic nature of the smaller merchants.

From the beginning, SONIMEX has been opposed by the
traditional suppliers in Dakar. It has had great difficulty in
acquiring credit from the local commercial bank, and then
only on onerous terms and in limited amounts. Accordingly,
it was not initially able to extend credit to merchants, as was
the custom of the Dakar importers, nor was it able to finance
sufficiently large stocks in the interior. Finally, it faced the

virtually uncontrolled imports of contraband from the open
borders to the north, south, and east. This had led to competition from illegally imported sugar and, at times, to the
probable export of SONIMEX tea to Senegal, where prices
were higher than were those in Mauritania. In general, coordination between the ONTP and SONIMEX was poor in the
important matter of establishing competitive prices for goods
at the point of consumption. Because of these difficulties, it
was not clear whether the national objectives of supplying
basic consumer goods at favorable prices were, in fact, being
achieved while both agencies operated.

SONIMEX plays an important role in Mauritania's economic
life, a role that could be considerably augmented. Basically,
the bulk of the country's inhabitants are engaged in traditional
rural occupations in the south and the east. Their main products are sold at low prices at the places of production, and
they must pay high prices for the basic staples of life that come
from other areas. The situation was exacerbated by lack of
local stocks and the opportunities for monopoly profits on the
part of the limited number of merchant houses that supplied
local retailers.

With the establishment of stocks at major consumption
points in the interior and with access to bank credit to purchase
stocks abroad and hold them in Mauritania, SONIMEX has been
able to harmonize prices of the commodities that it controls
and to improve the adequacy of supplies greatly, particularly
in the east. It still faces competition from contraband and has
not yet been able to develop a full system of giving credit to
its suppliers. In fact, it deals principally with some 200 large
merchants, who enjoy quantity discounts, have financing, and
are apparently able to still make speculative profits in the
isolated parts of the country.

Mauritania has a system of official price controls on
essential consumption goods that are based on local conditions.
Enforcement of price controls is, however, largely ineffective.
In order to reduce the price of sugar in the areas furthest
from Nouakchott and to establish a uniform national price, an
equalization fund was set up from the proceeds of the consumption tax. There is reluctance to apply the equalization principle
to all commodities, since this would eliminate the natural advantages of certain locations and could lead to a retardation
of economic development by artificially raising prices in some
regions and distorting investment decisions.

In the end, SONIMEX will only be able to perform its
functions of supplying basic consumer goods at reasonable

prices by adopting a policy of competing with imports in the border areas. As was seen in the discussion of millet, SONIMEX can also play a major role in improving the lot of the rural population by overcoming the distributional and marketing problems associated with millet-sorghum production and consumption.

WATER AND ELECTRICITY

During the first plan, an important effort was made to supply Nouakchott and Port-Etienne with water. Thus, although water shortages exist, the problem will be solved, for a time, upon the completion of works now under construction. As a result, no further new investments are contemplated in the second plan period for these two towns.

The Nouakchott water supply is operated by a semipublic company, the Société Mauritanienne d'Electricité (MAURELEC), that, in 1968, replaced a private company, the Société Africaine d'Electricité (SAFELEC), that was under contract to the government. A severe shortage of water limits daily consumption. The original water supply of the capital is from artesian wells located at Idini, 55 km. away, and carried by pipeline with a capacity of 1, 200 cubic meters. When it became apparent that a major expansion would be necessary, two solutions were considered. The first was to build a new, larger pipe to the same source at an average estimated cost of CFAF 80 per cubic meter of water, including both amortization and interest payments.

The second solution, which was adopted, was to build a somewhat experimental desalinization plant of 3, 400 cubic meters daily, at a total cost originally estimated at CFAF 850 million, but which probably exceeded CFAF 1, 000 million when it was completed, well behind schedule. The decision to construct this plant was based mainly on the fact that FAC originally offered a CFAF 500 million grant and a CFAF 250 million thirty-year loan at 1 per cent interest, plus an annual operating subsidy of CFAF 30 million. Additional FAC financing and suppliers' credits have raised the total investment to about CFAF 1.2 billion. It is reported that, even with these favorable terms, the cost of water is about CFAF 190 per cubic meter, which may be compared with a cost of CFAF 120 per cubic meter of water from the original pipeline. This plant, plus the existing system, was supposed to provide sufficient water to meet demand through 1974.

The rapid population growth of Nouakchott has caused demand for water to exceed supply, however. Plans call for increasing the flow from the wells at Idini to 6,000 cubic meters daily by hastily constructing a new pipeline financed with suppliers' credits. With continued population growth it may be necessary to carry out a second expansion to 20,000 cubic meters daily capacity within a decade. Consideration is even being given to bringing water from the Senegal River, over 200 km. away. Despite the shortage of water, SAFELEC had considerable difficulty in collecting bills. Some CFAF 50 million were reportedly in arrears, mainly from public agencies, in 1967.

Until 1969, water was provided to Port-Etienne by MIFERMA, which transported it in railroad tank cars from a source 84 km. away. The water was sold to the town at CFAF 650 per cubic meter. Daily consumption was some 1,000 cubic meters. With the rapid development of the fishing industry and its requirement for large amounts of water, the government decided to build a pipeline to the source, which, in its first phase, will supply some 3,000 cubic meters daily and which is sufficient to supply the town's needs through 1975. Half of this consumption would be for industrial uses. The pipeline and pumping installations cost CFAF 1.3 billion and were financed by a FED grant.

Electric power capacity in Nouakchott was 930 kw., resulting from some CFAF 250 million in investments during the first plan. In 1969, a new desalinization plant was expected to add another 500 kw. of firm capacity. With an estimated 10 per cent annual rise in consumption, this capacity was to have been sufficient to meet demand until 1972. The desalinization plant has not worked well, however, and demand rose faster than anticipated, causing a severe power shortage. Plans call for increasing the capacity of the power plant to 1,500 kw. with suppliers' credits and constructing a new diesel or steam plant of up to 4,000-kw. capacity, later.

Some 87 per cent of the country's installed capacity of 32,000 kw. belong to the two mining companies that supply the towns of Port-Etienne, Zouerate/F'Derik, and Akjoujt. In Port-Etienne, MIFERMA installed a capacity of 8,000 kw. in 1967. By agreement, MIFERMA delivered 1,000 kw. to the town at a reported price of CFAF 15 per kwh. The main center of mining operations at Zouerate has an installed capacity of some 11,000 kw. SOMIMA was to install a capacity of some 6,000 kw. at Akjoujt to provide for the needs of the copper mines and the town. Smaller public diesel plants

managed by MAURELEC exist at Atar, Rosso, and Kaedi.
The plant at Kaedi was expanded to provide for the needs of
the abattoir-refrigerator plant and the tannery. Consumer
prices for power range from CFAF 29 per kwh. for high-
voltage users to CFAF 34 per kwh. for low-voltage users.

CONSTRUCTION

The Sociétié d'Equipement de la Mauritanie (SEM) was
established in February, 1964, as successor to the Société
d'Urbanisme et de Construction Immobilière de Nouakchott
(SUCIN), a firm that had undertaken the contracting work
for the construction of the capital. About CFAF 3 billion
was financed by the Caisse Centrale and FAC. SEM was
established to study, supervise construction, and maintain
public and private installations of all kinds that would contribute
to the development of Mauritania. Rather typically, it represents another attempt to combine public and private capital to
achieve national objectives. The capital is CFAF 35 million,
of which the state holds CFAF 16 million, with the remainder
divided among such public enterprises as the BMD, the Social
Security Fund, (Caisse Nationale de Securité Sociale), and
such private enterprises as MIFERMA and the Société Centrale
pour l'Equipement du Territoire (SCET) Coopération.

Contracts for public accounts rose from CFAF 204 million in 1965 to CFAF 332 million in 1966. Despite this, the
company had too little work to make a profit. In part, this
was because of the reduction of construction in Nouakchott
connected with the completion of major buildings and the shortage of water. In part, it was due to the placing of maintenance
in the hands of the Ministry of Equipment in January, 1967,
which undertook this work for itself, and to the decision of the
Council of Ministers to separate the drawing up of plans, the
preparation of bids, and the supervision of their execution.

Nevertheless, although no longer in a virtual monopoly
position and suffering from what it regards as competition
from the Ministry of Equipment, SEM has received a good
deal of business from public and private sources. For
example, with financing from the BMD and the BIAO, it undertook the construction of buildings on a lease-purchase basis
for public and private organizations.

In August, 1966, the Social Security Administration
charged SEM with the construction of housing in Nouakchott

valued at CFAF 150 million. The company is also working
on a plan for the government to improve the slums surround-
ing the iron-mining town of Zouerate, as well as public projects, such as schools financed by the capital budget. It is
supervising the construction of the abattoir-refrigerator
plant and related electricity and water facilities at Kaedi
financed mainly by FAC.

8

Limited progress was made in education during the first plan period. From 1963 to 1966, primary enrollment rose from 18,200 to 20,400, or some 6,000 less than foreseen by the plan. This reduction from plan targets was caused by the necessity to reduce costs, by closing underutilized schools in sparsely populated areas, while concentrating educational resources in areas where minimum class sizes of twenty-five could be maintained. The planned improvement in the quality of education did not take place. On the contrary, a continuous lowering of the level of the teaching staff was registered.

In secondary education, the number of students enrolled rose faster than foreseen in the plan. By 1966-67, there were 1,900 students instead of the 1,520 anticipated. This rise was due to the unusually large number of students graduating from primary schools during this period. Entry standards were not sufficiently high, and the quality of secondary students in general, as well as the efficiency of the system, was lowered.

A number of new schools were opened. A technical lycée and college were opened in Nouakchott, although the first year had to be repeated because equipment was not made available on time. A primary teacher-training college was opened in Nouakchott in 1964. The first graduates graduated a year late, due to the closing of schools during disturbances that year.

In Port-Etienne, the Mamadou Touré teacher-training center was reorganized to provide vocational training, not only at the semiskilled or skilled level but also at the foreman and supervisor level. A section to train fishermen was added. In 1967, 168 trainees graduated, of whom seventy were from

short courses and the remainder from a nine-month course.
The output of this school appears to be adequate to meet demand, given that MIFERMA trains its own workers and
SOMIMA will do the same in the copper industry.* Employers
complain about the low quality of workers trained in the Port-
Etienne school and have suggested a two-year minimum course,
with periods set aside for apprenticeship training.

In 1965, an agricultural school was started in Kaedi,
financed by the United Nations Development Program (UNDP)
and administered by Food and Agriculture Organization (FAO)
experts. Two classes of thirty-eight and twenty-five, respectively, were begun in 1965 and 1966. In 1967, at the suggestion
of the IBRD mission a substantial change in curriculum was
adopted in order to enable the school to respond more effectively to the need for middle-level extension workers for the
rural development program. A National School of Public Administration was begun that has so far trained only lower-
level personnel.

In total, investments realized during the first plan period
amounted to CFAF 462 million, largely financed by FAC.
Allocations during this period amounted to some CFAF 855
million, of which some CFAF 570 million was from FAC and
the balance from FED. In terms of the current budget, the
Ministry of Education share rose from 12 per cent in 1962 to
16 per cent in 1966, excluding the centers at Port-Etienne
and Kaedi.

Although only some 15 per cent of the school-age population is in school, the resources that are devoted to education
are substantial, amounting to some 20 per cent of the current
budget. Account should also be taken of the considerable
number of Koranic schools, which teach elementary reading
and writing in Arabic throughout the country, although they
teach no subject matter. The system of education is not only
hampered by the wide dispersion of population but by the necessity to train students in both Arabic and French, a policy that
the government feels it must continue, even at the first grade
of elementary school. The Negroes in effect learn both Arabic
and French as foreign languages.

A good deal of applied research needs to be done before

---

*See R. Westebbe, Guidelines for a Four-Year Develop-
ment Program for Mauritania, "Report by 1967 IBRD Technical
Assistance Mission" (Washington, D. C.: IBRD, July, 1968),
Vol. II, Part II, chap. iii, for an analysis of the successful
MIFERMA school.

effective education programs can be devised for the nomadic
and peasant masses. At the higher levels, almost all education is in French, so as to establish equivalence with the
French system. There is also a great deficiency of well-
trained Arabic teachers. The type of education given in the
French-oriented secondary school does not respond well to
Mauritanian needs, nor is it of a sufficiently high quality.

The government will, apparently, consider suggested reforms designed to give more-practical training to the great
proportion of students who leave school before getting a
Baccalaureat Diplôme (BAC). A rapid expansion of secondary-
school students is required to meet the country's projected
requirements for trained manpower. In order to achieve this
expansion and reduce the high cost of boarding students, the
1970-73 plan calls for the construction, with foreign aid, of
seven secondary schools outside the capital. Reliance will
continue to be placed on technical assistance programs to
staff secondary schools until a teacher-training college being
financed by FAC gets under way.

9

FINANCE

PUBLIC FINANCE

The system of public accounting employed in Mauritania is an obstacle to the formulation of current economic policy, as well as to the achievement of development goals.   There are two principal reasons for this.   First, the way that the governmental financial system is organized makes it difficult, if not impossible, to determine the economic impact of the budget or even the volume of resources available for development and nondevelopment purposes.   In brief, the budget does not distinguish between development and nondevelopment outlays, between current and capital outlays, and between cash and administrative transactions.   A feature of the current, or ordinary, budget is the wide discretion given the Ministry of Finance to determine how much revenue will be shown in the published budget exercises for each year, so as to control more effectively demands for expenditures.   The system is so complicated that only a handful of officials in the Ministry of Finance and the Treasury fully understand the meaning of the figures.

The Treasury is the government's fiscal agent and banker. It receives and disburses funds prescribed in the budget and by the Ministry of Finance.   It is the depository of the accounts of most, although not all, public bodies.   For example, the large and increasing social security system reserves are kept mainly in a private commercial bank.   The Treasury also operates the Caisse de Reserve, or government Reserve Fund,

which is used from time to time to finance both the current
and the capital budgets and which has received only the surpluses of the current budget, after receipt of the French subsidy, as a source of funds in recent years. The capital budget
is prepared by the Ministry of Planning and Rural Development
and essentially contains investment and other outlays that
could not be financed in the current budget. Its principal
source of finance has been French Government subsidies,
through FAC, that are tied to specific purposes that could not
be financed under normal FAC criteria for development projects in Mauritania.

In order to see the government budget in perspective, it
would be useful to discuss the entire public sector. This
consists of the current and capital budgets of the central
government, in excess of twenty special funds, and eight regional administrations enjoying limited autonomy with respect
to some 10 per cent of the central government's current budget.
There are also a number of public and semipublic agencies,
such as the Social Security Fund, the Post Office (Office de
Post et Télégraphe, OPT), Air Mauritanie, and the port, rail,
and radio organizations.

The current budget includes transfers to cover the deficits
of the post and telegraph system, as well as subsidies to the
local communities. The government also is a major share-
holder in the defunct Société Mauritanienne d'Armement à la
Pêche (SOMAP) and Société Mauritanienne des Industries de
la Pêche (SOMIP) fishing companies, as well as the guarantor
of their debts. SOMIP is attempting to service its debts from
the rental income on its fishmeal factory, while the SOMAP
debt is being financed by selling fishing rights to foreign companies. It is estimated that about half of the central government's current and capital outlays do not pass through the
budgets, excluding independent and semi-independent enterprises. A good part of these nonbudgeted expenditures concern
foreign aid.

The second reason that public finances constitute an obstacle to economic policy formulation and the achievement of
development goals is the sheer inadequacy of budgetary resources. Not only are resources inadequate to provide sufficient financing for present recurrent development-related
outlays and for nondevelopment social and administrative
purposes, but public savings are not sufficient to provide a
local currency contribution for capital investment purposes.
Accordingly, even the maintenance of the present level of
development presents difficulties, to say nothing of the financing
of a large additional development program.

In the analysis that follows, the current budget and the
capital budget will be dealt with separately and then in consolidated form, together with their relation to the Treasury
and to other sources of financing.

The Current Budget

The basic budgetary process is designed to create an
equilibrium between receipts and expenditures for a calendar-
year exercise that is the annual budget approved and amended
by the legislature. The first estimate made by the Ministry
of Finance is of expenses for the year. Receipts are then
estimated by department in the Ministry of Finance. Estimated
expenses are pruned in order to match estimated receipts,
and legislative approval is obtained, usually in the fall.

In November of each year, tax declarations are accumulated, and an estimate is made of receipts by department for
the year and of the deficit or surplus likely to occur in relation
to the quota of revenue that was to be collected by each department according to the budget. By the end of the year, final
budgetary revisions approved by the National Assembly are
available. On the basis of estimated receipts and revised expenditures, each department engages in a procedure that essentially allows it to allocate receipts after December 31 to
the previous or the new year's budget in order to make available the amount of receipts that it is supposed to provide.

In the case of the department "Contributions Diverse, "
one of the most important in the Ministry of Finance, the
books are closed on January 31 of each year. For example,
if this department requires CFAF 100 million to meet its
quota as of December 31, it may divide tax receipts and
declarations made during January in order to allocate CFAF
100 million to the previous year and the balance to the new
year. Thus, the department of Contributions Diverse shows
receipts on a January 31 to January 31 basis. After December
31, no expenditures are made for the budget year unless a
legal obligation for this was created during the year prior to
December 31. Similarly, certified tax obligations to pay are
the basis for assigning payments received after December 31
to a given budget year.

The Treasury follows a different system from that of the
individual tax departments. It closes its books for a given
budget year on March 31 of each year. All payments received
by March 31 for declarations of the previous budget year are

assigned to the so-called exercices anterieur's in the next
year's accounts. These exercices anterieurs amounted to
some CFAF 200 million in 1968. For any given year, the receipts "anterieurs" are the sum of amounts not collected in
previous budget years. Tax declarations and payments for
the current budget year made in January, February, and
March of the next year are, in principle, counted in the current year. Thus, in the first three months of a calendar year,
in effect, two budgetary exercises are in operation.

From 1960 through 1969, current budget expenditures
rose from CFAF 3.0 billion to CFAF 6.2 billion, while receipts rose from CFAF 1.0 billion to CFAF 5.8 billion. (See
Table 13.) In order to analyze these developments, it is desirable to consider fiscal developments in terms of the periods
1960-63, 1963-66, and 1966-69. The development of actual
receipts and expenditures in million CFAF for budget exercise
years 1960, 1963, 1966, and 1969 is as follows:

	1960	1963	1966	1969*
Current Receipts	1,041	3,413	4,746	5,829
Current Expenditures	3,038	4,287	4,390	6,220
	-1,997	-874	356	-391

A further freedom in transferring receipts between budget
years existed until 1968 because of the taxes received annually
from MIFERMA under the long-term tax scheme and the levies
paid on ore extracted. These were considered outside the
budget and are shown as receipts for another budget year. In
1964, receipts from this source were actually CFAF 780
million. The budget for that year shows receipts of only CFAF
630 million. The balance of CFAF 102 million was transferred
to the 1967 budget.

In the first period (1960-63), receipts rose from CFAF
1 billion to CFAF 3.4 billion. Of this 2.4 billion rise in current revenues, close to CFAF 600 million was in the form of
direct taxes, and over CFAF 1.2 billion was in the form of
indirect taxes. MIFERMA contributed some CFAF 500 million
in addition. In this period, the principal reason for the rise
in revenues was the introduction of turnover taxes and the imposition of higher income-tax rates. At the end of 1962,
Mauritania negotiated a rise from 5 per cent to 8.66 per cent

_____

*These figures may be revised. Expenditures do not in-
clude over CFAF 200 million in unpaid bills.

TABLE 13

Current Budget, 1960-69
(Billion CFAF)

Item	1960	1963	1966	1969*
Revenue				
Direct taxes	.3	.8	.9	1.2
MIFERMA taxation	-	.5	1.6	1.4
Indirect taxation	.7	1.9	1.9	2.5
Other	-	.2	.3	.7
Total	1.0	3.4	4.7	5.8
Expenditures				
Salaries	1.4	2.3	2.5	3.6
Maintenance	.2	.1	.1	.1
Materials & supplies	1.0	1.2	.9	1.8
Transfers & subsidies	.3	.6	.5	.5
Public debt	.1	.1	.4	.5
Unclassified	-	-	-	-
Total	3.0	4.3	4.4	6.5*

*Based in part on budget estimates subject to revision.

Source: RIM Ministry of Finance.

of its share of the total imports entering the Senegal-Mauritania Customs Union.

On the expenditure side, total current outlays rose from CFAF 3.0 billion in 1960 to CFAF 4.3 billion in 1963. Personnel outlays accounted for some CFAF 800 million of this, and expenditures for materials and equipment contributed less than CFAF 300 million. Maintenance outlays fell, and transfer payments rose. In this period, the entire expense of the security forces was assumed by the government, as French forces withdrew from the country. The state also assumed other outlays connected with the establishment of a new government.

The financing of the current budget deficit was, in an over-all sense, almost entirely from French budget subsidies, since the accumulated deficit of some CFAF 6 billion was more than covered by amounts received from France, which totaled some CFAF 7 billion in this period. The Reserve Fund was augmented by the transfer of sizeable budget surpluses from the late 1950's and, in turn, disbursed funds to the current budget during certain budget years, which, in conjunction with the French subsidies, led to surpluses that were transferred back to the Reserve Fund.

In the second period (1963-66), fiscal policy underwent a major change as a result of the government's decision in 1963 to forego in the future the French subsidy to the current budget. The decision, which followed the introduction of a new four-year development plan, required the imposition of a policy of drastic budgetary austerity. The deficit in the current budget was CFAF 1 billion in 1963, according to the published figures. The decision was politically unpopular as it involved limiting the numbers and compensation of government employees. The number of Ministers were reduced and members of the assembly no longer received a salary.

New taxes were levied on imports and consumption goods. The yield from these taxes, particularly the meat tax, was less than anticipated, resulting in a failure to balance the 1964 budget. The budget for that year indicates that personnel outlays were stabilized in 1964, and materials and maintenance outlays were cut sharply. (See Appendix Table 10.) Although expenditures were drastically curtailed in 1964, the pressures to take on new government employees, particularly school graduates and returnees from abroad, led to an unexpected expansion of personnel outlays. In part, this rise also reflects higher compensation and normal increases in the cost of the existing civil service.

Expenditures for materials did not return to 1963 levels until 1968, while maintenance outlays rose only in 1964 over the 1963 level. Outlays for maintenance remain far below the amounts required to maintain the existing stock of public capital goods. It is estimated that maintenance outlays for roads alone should amount to over CFAF 200 million annually on the basis of the present road network. The costs of security services are quite heavy. They absorbed 22.7 per cent of budgetary resources in 1968, compared with 10.3 per cent in 1960. (See Appendix Table 10.)

On the receipt side, current revenues rose by CFAF 1.3 billion during the second period (1963-66), of which less than CFAF 102 million was in direct taxes and over CFAF 1 billion in taxes from MIFERMA. This sharp rise in revenues, particularly from MIFERMA, has permitted surpluses in the current budget to be achieved for the years 1965-68. In 1964

and 1965, a major and largely successful effort was undertaken to collect tax arrears. The surplus in the budget for
1965 reflects part of the actual rise in receipts from this
source.

In the third period (1966-69), a sharp rise in current outlays took place. By 1969, revenues had slowed down, mainly
due to lagging MIFERMA payments, and a large current-
account budget deficit was recorded, after several years of
current budget surpluses. Current expenditures rose by 12
per cent in 1967, 8 per cent in 1968, and an estimated 20 per
cent in 1969. The increase after 1966 was due about equally
to higher wage and salary payments and expenditures for
materials and supplies (See Table 13.)

In 1966, a 5 per cent cost-of-living allowance was given
to civil servants in the capital. In 1967, the retirement age
for government employees was reduced from 55 to 50 years
of age. Finally, wage and salary payments rose through upgrading of personnel, from 48 per cent of current expenditures
in 1962 to 56 per cent in 1968. In 1966, materials and supplies had been cut to austerity levels as a result of 10 per
cent across-the-board cuts in equipment outlays; thus, the
rise in this category through 1968 was, in effect, a restora-
tion of essential supplies for current operations. Even so,
by 1968, materials and supplies accounted for only 23 per
cent of total current expenditures, compared with 32 per cent
in 1960, and were probably valued at less in real terms in
1968.

The sharp rise in expenditures in the 1969 budget resulted
from further increases in the wage and salary and materials
and supplies categories. In terms of functional categories,
the current budget in the 1960's showed a marked tendency
for army and police outlays to rise from about 10 per cent of
total current expenditures to 25 per cent. * Education has
also absorbed an increasing proportion of total current outlays.
Given the high per pupil cost of educating a dispersed population, this category probably leads to decreasing social returns.
A better organized and more relevant educational system,
which is contemplated, would, however, make good use of
additional resources. Since the bulk of the population lives
in the rural sector, the fact that current outlays have probably

_____

*At the January, 1968, Party Congress, the army was
designated as a "popular army" and was charged with assisting
local public works, although no budgetary allocation was
identified with this task.

not even increased in proportion to price rises is rather surprising. The government services supported by allocations
in this sector have steadily declined in effectiveness as a
result.

Annual revenue increases ranged from 10 per cent to 14
per cent between 1966 and 1968. (See Appendix Table 12.)
In 1967, consumption (principally sugar) and excise-tax increases accounted for most of the rise. In 1968, this category
more than doubled again, mainly due to sugar taxes. The
Ministry of Finance intends to simplify the fiscal code. A
Bureau of Studies was set up to provide analyses of the economic
and fiscal impacts of changing the tax structure.

Some three-fourths of Mauritania's current revenues including Milerma are from indirect taxes. Import duties and
export taxes from mining concerns account for about 30 per
cent of total indirect revenues and import duties about 20 per
cent. Consumption and excise taxes account for a further 15
per cent. Mauritania does not freely set its custom duties and
import taxes. These must conform to the terms of Mauritania's
association with the EEC and with its membership in the
UNDEAO (Union Douanière). Until the end of 1969, Mauritania and Senegal also had a customs union, which gave Mauritania 8.66 per cent of the customs duties and import taxes
collected in both countries under the common external tariff.
Mauritania maintained that its fair share of the common receipts should be higher, preferably in the neighborhood of 15
per cent.

Imports are subject to different scales of charges. The
minimum tariff ranges from 2 per cent to 75 per cent of the
cost, insurance, and freight (c.i.f.) value of imports from
most-favored-nation countries, except EEC and UNDEAO
members. The general tariff is three times the minimum.
EEC and UNDEAO countries became subject, on February 1,
1970, to import taxes and fiscal duties at rates of 56 per
cent of those applicable to other countries; the rate may be
raised to 70 per cent for a UNDEAO member wanting to protect
a particular industry.

Mauritania also levies a fiscal duty, which usually falls
within the 5 per cent to 20 per cent range of all imports, and
a statistical tax of 2 per cent on the c.i.f. value of all imports, except some food products and capital equipment.
There is also an import tax, which ranges between 20 per cent
and 30 per cent for most goods, except food and capital goods,
and, finally, an import turnover tax, which is levied on the
c.i.f. value, including custom duties and import taxes, which
ranges from 12 per cent to 25 per cent, and which applies to

most goods, defined by categories of luxury, except basic
foodstuffs and industrial raw materials. * This complicated
system of import levies accounted for some 26 per cent of
total current revenues in the 1965-68 period.

Tax revenues from MIFERMA accounted for about one-
fourth of total current revenues in the same period and are
expected to decline as a percentage of the total as output and
exports level off. The copper mines are not expected to produce any significant resources for the budget until after the
mid-1970's. Sugar is subject to an excise tax of CFAF
18,371 a ton, and tea to a consumption tax of CFAF 100,000
a ton, which goes into a tea fund. Consumer taxes on tea,
tobacco, and, principally, sugar amounted to 12 per cent of
revenues in 1968.

Direct taxes are the only other important source of
government current revenues. Revenue from that source declined from 21 per cent of total current receipts in 1965 to a
little over 18 per cent in 1968. Despite the rises in national
income, wages, and salaries, income-tax revenues fell
slightly from CFAF 963 million to CFAF 954 million in this
period. The wage and salary tax ranges from 6 per cent on
monthly earnings of CFAF 6,000 to 15 per cent for monthly
earnings in excess of CFAF 70,000. Corporations pay a 25
per cent tax on profits and a 16 per cent tax on distributed
dividends. The mining companies are subject to special long-
term fiscal conventions. Unincorporated enterprises and
professions pay taxes ranging from 10 per cent to 15 per cent
on profits ranging from CFAF 100,000 and CFAF 300,000.

A general income tax on total taxable revenue ranges
from 2 per cent on annual incomes above CFAF 100,000 to
60 per cent for incomes in excess of CFAF 5 million. The
direct tax system has not shown much elasticity with respect
to incomes, which indicates that a review of collection procedures is in order. Government forecasts indicate that substantial increases are expected from this source, although a
basic study of the tax structure must still be done before
fundamental reforms can be undertaken. In general, Mauritania's total tax burden does not exceed 13 per cent of the
GDP at factor cost, which is less than that for neighboring
Mali (about 15 per cent) and substantially less than that for

---

*For a fuller description of the import levy and tax system,
see Surveys of African Economies, Vol. III: Mauritania
(Washington, D.C.: International Monetary Fund, 1970), pp.
354-62.

Senegal and the Ivory Coast (about 20 per cent), which have
admittedly richer economies.

In considering Mauritania's budgetary projections, account must be taken of two apparently conflicting tendencies.
On the one hand, requests of the services for budgetary allocations consistently exceed, in total, the amounts actually allocated by 20 per cent or more. The total volume of budgetary
outlays is, in effect, determined by estimated total revenues.
Since three-fourths of revenues are derived from indirect
taxes, including MIFERMA, the degree of flexibility in total
revenues is small and depends largely on changes in economic
activity. Direct taxes are collected from a relatively small
class of people and cannot expand rapidly, except for one-time
improvements in collection. On the other hand, government
services have often been unable to absorb all of the reduced
budgetary allocations made available. Absorptive capacity
is limited by lack of qualified personnel and inadequate coordination. Since the fiscal authorities tend to underestimate
revenues, the result is often the appearance of large current
surpluses, even when balanced current budgets are projected,
while urgent and high-priority expenditures are not accomplished.

The Capital Budget

The capital budget was originally intended to become the
governments' investment budget, according to the first four-
year plan. The refusal of the main outside financing agencies,
FAC and FED, to disburse their grants through this budget
has considerably restricted the role of the capital budget in
development, however. In effect, the capital budget has been
the recipient of French budget-balancing grants through FAC
when the French subsidy to the current budget was discontinued
at the request of the Mauritanian Government in 1963. The
sums allocated for this purpose rose from CFAF 700 million
in 1964 to CFAF 1 billion in 1965 and have been declining ever
since. In 1967, CFAF 300 million were anticipated. These
grants were sharply reduced in 1969. (Actual disbursements
are shown in Appendix Table 14.)

Projects that FAC would ordinarily refuse to finance
under the criteria of its regular development program in
Mauritania are included in the capital budget. If these receive
FAC approval for financing through a grant to the capital budget,
they are included in this budget. In addition, the government

has included miscellaneous outlays, such as a subsidy for the People's Party and certain maintenance expenditures, in this budget. Because expenditures have lagged behind allocations of grants, the capital budget has had a large carry-over of funds from year to year since 1963. These funds are earmarked for specific projects approved by FAC. In view of these large carry-overs, it must be presumed that the drawings of the capital budget from the Reserve Fund must have been for purposes for which FAC approval could not be obtained, but which the government nevertheless wanted to finance.

The capital budget, unlike the current budget, is never closed. Expenditures that occur during a calendar year are shown for the year in question, and financing obtained is carried forward, as indicated above, when not used in the year that it is made available. It is not clear where FAC funds carried forward are deposited. They do not appear in the Treasury accounts and are presumably retained by FAC for disbursement against approved vouchers. The major purposes for which expenditures were undertaken are set forth in Table 14.

The significance of this budget for the development program is marginal, for the bulk of investments are financed and supervised directly by FAC and FED. The capital budget is thus residual, containing projects that FAC cannot finance under its normal criteria, as well as outlays that the government could not finance under the current budget. In 1964, the drastic austerity imposed on the current budget led to certain items being transferred to the capital budget.

Following the ending of the French subsidy to the current budget in 1963, a program of direct subsidies by FAC to the capital budget was begun. From 1963 through 1968, total expenditures on the capital budget amounted to some CFAF 3.2 billion, and French subsidies to 2.3 billion. The capital budget received drawings from the reserve funds in the shortfall. (See Appendix Table 13.)

The figures budgeted for capital purposes annually often vary greatly from the budget outcome. The size of new allocations to this budget are clearly related to the amount of grants that FAC would be willing to provide for agreed-upon purposes. The financing of the capital budget was augmented by a larger transfer from the current budget in 1968, as well as the crediting of it with the proceeds from the Mauritanian share of the liquidation of MICUMA, the former copper concessionnaire. The 1967 capital budget, however, received CFAF 88.5 million

TABLE 14

Government Capital Budget Expenditures, 1960-68
(Million CFAF)

Expenditure	1960	1961	1962	1963	1964	1965	1966	1967[a]	1968
Infrastructure	84	109	264	221	235	137	270	143	103
Buildings (administrative &	129	26	388	167	158	100	420	337	327
residential)	-	-	-	-	-	-	32	26	19
Participations	51	-	-	136	14	20	39	157	67
Local authorities	-	-	-	-	-	-	10	25	21
Miscellaneous (including maintenance, contributions, subsidies)	17	11	-	-	21[b]	34[b]	-	-	1
Total	281	146	652	524	428	291	771	686	538

[a]Original budget estimates included a CFAF 25 million subsidy for the Peoples' Party.
[b]Maintenance.

Source: RIM, Ministry of Finance.

in advances from SOMIMA to finance public works at Akjoujt, whereas only CFAF 5 million was budgeted for this purpose in 1968. The carry-over of undisbursed funds for the capital budget rose on a provisional basis to CFAF 766 million as of the end of 1967.

THE TREASURY

The Treasury is the government's fiscal agent. It collects all revenues and makes all payments in accordance with the budget. It further allocates receipts within legal limits by budget year, in order to present a budgetary picture as prescribed by the Ministry of Finance.

The Treasury is also the government's banker. It receives deposits from most of the public organizations and maintains a Reserve Fund that finances the government's current and capital budgets, although its sole source of income has been the current budget surpluses. (The operations of this Reserve Fund are shown in Appendix Table 14.) During the period 1960-66, the Reserve Fund received a total of CFAF 1,853 million from surpluses in the current budget, some dating back to 1958. It disbursed 1,071 million to the current budget in this period and CFAF 636 million to the capital budget. In 1966, a surplus of CFAF 391.5 million was registered from the 1965 current budget, and CFAF 287 million was disbursed to the capital budget.

By the end of 1966, the resources of the Reserve Fund had been reduced to CFAF 189 million, which made it appear unlikely that it would be able to provide any important amount of financing for the deficits of either operating budgets in the future. This presumably explains the inclusion of loans from other sources, such as the Treasury and the Banque Centrale des Etats de l'Afrique de l'Ouest (BCEAO) in the provisional 1966 and 1967 budgets. The generation of a large current surplus in 1966, however, replenished the Reserve Fund. By the end of 1967, it showed a balance of CFAF 516 million, which had declined to CFAF 201 million following the budget deficit of 1969.

Aside from the limited borrowing facilities from the French Treasury, the Mauritanian Treasury has large deposits from public agencies, the available cash balances of which could be used to finance government operations. At the end of 1966, these deposits totaled over CFAF 700 million,

mainly from the Post Office, the Civil Service pension fund,
and the communities. By the end of 1969, these deposits had
risen to CFAF 1.031 million. In 1966, some CFAF 700 million were deposited by the Treasury with the BIAO and the
BMD, the latter on a long-term basis. By the end of 1967,
the Treasury had CFAF 396 million on deposit with the BIAO
at 4 per cent interest. The Social Security Fund deposits
were deposited directly with the BIAO and amounted to CFAF
334 million at the end of 1966. Government deposits with de-
posit-money banks rose from CFAF 450 million in 1966 to
CFAF 734 million in 1967 and declined to CFAF 478 million
by the end of 1969.

In 1968, the Finance Law included a number of special
Treasury accounts as annexes to the budget, including a number of income-producing social funds, as well as the new fund
for losses on drafts guaranteed by the government. In total,
the government is authorized to exceed special-account receipts by CFAF 308 million, to be covered from Treasury
resources. This deficit is mainly attributed to losses on imported millet (CFAF 112 million), advances to various public
bodies and collectivities (CFAF 30 million), and losses on
government-guaranteed drafts (CFAF 60 million).

The Finance Law for 1968 also authorizes the government
to contract a CFAF 200 million loan with the Caisse Centrale
for the water and electricity systems of Nouakchott and Port-
Etienne and to increase the capital of SOMAP. In addition, a
loan from the French Government, through FAC, of CFAF
70 million is authorized for various projects in the fishing
industry. The government may also guarantee foreign suppliers' credits contracted by the BMD for various organizations
and governments up to CFAF 300 million, as well as CFAF
100 million in loans by the BMD to public enterprises and
mixed companies. Finally, the Ministry of Finance is authorized to cover short-term needs from the BCEAO.

The problems of financing government budgetary and nonbudgetary outlays became increasingly difficult as the decade
of the 1960's drew to a close. In the first half of the decade,
average annual current budget expenditures exceeded revenues
by about CFAF 1 billion, and public capital outlays added
another CFAF 2 billion to financing requirements. Grant aid
to the budget from France and, to a lesser extent, from FED
covered almost all of the requirements, leaving only a frac-
tional amount for Treasury financing.

In the second part of the decade, from 1965 to 1968, the
current budget, on an average annual basis, moved into a

slight surplus of some CFAF 400 million, which covered part
of the total public capital spending of some CFAF 2.5 billion
in this period.   Foreign aid in the form of subsidies to the
capital budget--FED aid and, more recently, IBRD/IDA
loans--more than covered financing requirements and enabled
an average annual net contribution of some CFAF 200 million
to be made to the Treasury.

By 1969, however, the reappearance of a large current
deficit of some CFAF 600 million, coupled with budgetary
and nonbudgetary capital spending totaling some CFAF 4.7
billion, increased total government financing requirements
to CFAF 5.3 billion.   The French subsidy to the capital budget
had practically disappeared, and other forms of project aid--
from FED and the IBRD--amounted to only 3.0 billion.   The
government was forced to contract for short-term suppliers'
credits for about CFAF 1.1 billion to run up accounts payable
and to call on the Treasury for some CFAF 1 billion.   (See
Appendix Table 13.)

As Table 15 makes clear, the drawdown of Treasury
liquid assets in 1969 was possible because of the steady increase in deposits by special pension funds and public agencies.
The increased resources from these sources will not be sufficient to sustain, for long, deficits in government operations
of the size experienced in 1969 and projected in 1970.

There will also come a point when these deposits with the
Treasury will have to be used for their originally intended
purposes.   The use of suppliers' credits to finance a good
part of recent budgets will also place an added burden on
budgets during the new plan period.   A serious challenge thus
faces the government in augmenting net public savings to
complement whatever foreign aid it can acquire for the purpose
of financing the increased levels of development expenditures
projected.

THE MONETARY SYSTEM

The Mauritanian banking system consists of two com-
mercial banks--the BIAO and the Société Mauritanienne de
Banque (SMB), a newly established branch of the French
Société Générale--the BMD, and the local branch of the
BCEAO.   The monetary system is part of the West African

TABLE 15

Treasury Balance Sheets, 1966-69
(Billion CFAF, ending December 31)

Item	1966	1967	1968	1969
Assets				
Liquid	0. 7	1. 1	0. 9	0. 4
Advances to regional				
treasuries	0. 6	0. 7	0. 7	0. 9
Total	1. 3	1. 8	1. 6	1. 3
Liabilities				
Postal checking deposits	0. 3	0. 3	0. 4	0. 2
Public-agency deposits	0. 4	0. 5	0. 7	1. 2
Unpaid bills	-	0. 1	0. 1	0. 1
Balance budgetary				
operations	0. 6	0. 9	0. 4	-0. 2
Total	1. 3	1. 8	1. 6	1. 3

Source: RIM, Treasury.

Monetary Union, * as well as of the franc area. By agreement
with France, the Mauritanian franc and all other francs of
the monetary union are freely convertible into French francs.
Bank notes issued in Mauritania are legal tender in all other
CFA countries of the union and are distinguishable from the
others only by a separate letter on each note.

The BCEAO is administered by a Board of Directors representing all the member countries and France. Credit to
individual governments may not exceed 10 per cent of budgetary
receipts of the previous year; this may, in exceptional cases,
be raised to 15 per cent. In addition, the board establishes
ceilings for short- and medium-term credits to the private
sector and fixes rediscount ceilings for the individual firms.
The local BCEAO committee advises the board on these ceilings. Because of limited demand on the part of credit-worthy
borrowers, these ceilings, in the case of Mauritania, had no
significance until 1968. Advances to the government may

*The other members of the union are Dahomey, the Ivory
Coast, Niger, Senegal, Togo, and Upper Volta.

normally not exceed 240 days. The BCEAO requires commercial banks to keep a 70 per cent liquidity ratio between their liquid assets and their short-term liabilities; this ratio will rise to 75 per cent by 1970/71. Credit institutions are also subject to solvency ratios.

The West African Monetary Union also fixed interest rates for various classes of transactions. The basic discount rate for the BCEAO is 3.5 per cent; a preferential rate of 3 per cent is applicable to exports outside the BCEAO area. Short-term interest rates vary from 4.5 per cent to 5.25 per cent on credits to public enterprises for crop financing to 9 per cent for credits for enterprises in excess of the set ceiling for that firm and where the credit exceeds CFAF 5 million. Medium-term credits carry rates of from 5.5 per cent to 8.5 per cent. The BMD may charge 4 per cent to 5 per cent for long-term socially desirable loans and up to 9 per cent for private luxury construction loans. Time and savings deposit rates vary from 3.5 per cent to 4.5 per cent, depending on the amount.

Each of the member countries maintains a balance with the BCEAO. The French Government guarantees to convert this CFAF balance freely into French francs for the purpose of making payments outside the zone. In this case, interest rate penalties are applied, and the credit facilities of the BCEAO to a member country may be curtailed. In the case of Mauritania, which has an over-all external surplus, these measures have had no applicability. In essence, the monetary union prevents individual member countries from exercising an independent monetary policy. Inflationary financing through the banking system is thereby prevented.

The sole commercial bank until 1967 was a branch of a French bank, the BIAO. It received private and official deposits and granted short-term credits to private commerce and industry, as well as to SONIMEX. In general, since the bank was not able to find sufficient eligible borrowers under its conservative criteria, the bulk of its deposits was placed in Paris. At the end of 1966, the BIAO had total domestic deposits of CFAF 2.2 billion, of which CFAF 800 million represented government deposits, including those of the BMD, and CFAF 1.1 billion were private demand deposits. Some CFAF 1.4 billion of the bank's assets were located abroad. The BIAO extended a CFAF 800 million documentary line of credit to SONIMEX under government guarantee, including control of warehouse stocks and a deposit of CFAF 200 million of the government's sugar subsidy fund as further guarantees.

Finally, the BIAO has the agreement of the BCEAO to rediscount this credit.

The second commercial bank, the SMB, was set up in
1967 at the invitation of the government for the purpose of increasing competition in banking and, thus, to make it easier
for Mauritanian merchants to get credit for shipments through
Nouakchott instead of through Dakar.

A major expansion in commercial bank activities took
place after 1967, due to the requirements of traders, including
SONIMEX, for financing goods that were previously imported
through Dakar and financed by banks there. Between the end
of 1966 and 1969, total credit to the private sector rose from
CFAF 1.4 billion to CFAF 5.1 billion. (See Table 16.) Trade
credit accounted for some CFAF 1 billion of this rise. The
demand for credit also rose on the part of the fishing industry,
where the output of the freezing plants was growing. Con-
struction-company credit rose by some CFAF 650 million
from the end of 1966 through mid-1969, largely in connection
with contracts let at the Akjoujt copper-mining installation
and then declined to 430 million by the end of 1969. Transport
credit also expanded, in connection with copper mining, as
did credit to mining. (See Appendix Table 15.)

In 1966, deposits from all sources were close to double
bank credits. By the end of 1969, deposits were only 60 per
cent of credits to the private sector, despite a threefold
growth in time and savings deposits and a 40 per cent rise in
demand deposits in this period. A good part of the rise in
domestic credit was financed by drawing down assets abroad
from CFAF 1.3 billion in 1966 to CFAF 126 million by the end
of 1969. By the end of 1968, the banks were forced to make
use of rediscount facilities at the BCEAO. By the end of 1969,
these rediscounts amounted to CFAF 1.3 billion.

The BMD, established in 1961, had in 1967, total assets
of some CFAF 1 billion, of which the Caisse Centrale has
contributed some CFAF 370 million in capital and loans. Out
of total short-term deposits of CFAF 400 million, the government Treasury has contributed about CFAF 250 million. The
equity capital of the BMD consists of CFAF 200 million, of
which CFAF 116 million was contributed by the government
(58 per cent) and the rest by the Caisse Centrale (CFAF 68
million) and the BCEAO (CFAF 16 million). The minority
shareholders exercise a veto power over all BMD loan operations, a feature that is, in part, responsible for the failure to
mount a more aggressive development loan policy. The minority
shareholders also exercise a veto over new sources of funds

TABLE 16

Assets and Liabilities of Commercial Banks and the BMD, 1962-69
(Million CFAF, end of period)

Item	1962	1963	1964	1965	1966	December, 1967	December, 1968	December, 1969
Assets								
Cash	96	75	69	101	76	125	252	149
Foreign assets	1,244	936	486	694	1,340	949	398	126
Claims on private sector								
Short-term	1,084	705	866	1,136	1,025	2,101	3,466	4,125
Medium-term	214	143	142	106	106	262	343	--
Long-term	--	100	254	282	258	230	189	--
Total claims on private sector	1,298	948	1,262	1,524	1,389	2,593	3,998	5,052
Assets = liabilities	2,638	1,959	1,817	2,319	2,805	3,667	4,648	5,327
Liabilities								
Demand deposits	640	906	691	769	1,505	1,755	2,217	2,060
Time & savings deposits	68	50	50	160	200	386	397	623
Government deposits	1,270	798	520	657	450	734	668	478
Foreign liabilities	--	159	331	564	423	552	677	631
Credit from BCEAO	662	94	24	--	--	--	334	1,348
Other items (net)	-2	-48	201	169	227	240	354	187

Sources: IMF, International Financial Statistics; BCEAO, Notes d'Information et Statistiques; and data provided by the BCEAO.

for the BMD. It is reported that this was the reason for the
rejection of an offer of a 1 million Deutschmark (DM), untied,
3 per cent, fifteen-year German loan for relending to Mauritanian borrowers.

At the end of September, 1967, the Caisse Centrale had
contributed CFAF 240 million in long-term advances and 20
million in medium-term advances. A further CFAF 587 million in short-term deposits were on hand, of which CFAF
453 million were from the Treasury of the government; the
balance came mainly from various insurance companies and
cooperatives. Total short-term deposits rose by CFAF 187
million during 1966/67, mainly from Treasury sources.
BMD loans at the end of September, 1967, consisted of CFAF
590 million of loans divided as follows:

Million CFAF

Agriculture	30
Handicraft, industry, & fishing	227*
Commerce	150
Housing	165
Other	18
Total	590

In the year ending September 30, 1967, loans rose by CFAF
60 million, mainly to commerce and, to a lesser extent, to
agriculture and handicrafts. A small loss was incurred on
operations in 1966, and the BMD just broke even in 1967.

The BMD administration contends that, in the absence of
adequately organized cooperatives and acceptable guarantees,
a good part of its financing has had to be devoted to the fishing
industry and to the construction of private housing and other
buildings, mainly for officials in Nouakchott. Bad and questionable debts on these accounts already amounted to CFAF
65 million in 1967. Agricultural credits constituted less than
5 per cent of total loans. Some CFAF 483 million of the
BMD's assets were deposited with the BIAO as of September
30, 1967.

By September 30, 1969, the BMD had total loans outstanding as follows:

---

*Information obtained by the 1967 IBRD mission indicates
that the BMD had lent CFAF 175 million to a fish-freezing
plant and had participated in the SOMIP-SOMAP fishing companies in the amount of CFAF 20 million.

Million CFAF

Agriculture	45
Manufacturing, industry, & fishing	599
Housing	408
Consumer credit	146
Government entities	96
Total	1, 294

Although the categories do not fully correspond with those for 1967, it is clear that housing and consumer credit received a considerable part of the expansion of credit. Further, over one-third of total credit was short term. The BMD suffered losses in the Nema ploughing project, in the fishing industry, and in manufacturing that have eaten up one-third of its capital. The financing of the fishing industry was at least in accord with the development purposes for which the BMD was established, no matter how badly the industry itself was organized. The substantial credits to private housing and to consumers are not developmental in nature. Operations of the BMD have reportedly declined, as it has been unable to find sufficient qualified projects for financing.

10

FOREIGN TRADE
PAYMENTS
AND
INVESTMENT

FOREIGN TRADE

The balance of payments does not constitute a constraint
to development, nor is it particularly important in the formulation of current economic policy, because the country's external accounts are inherently strong by virtue of its position
as a large mineral and cattle exporter. In addition, Mauritania's membership in the West African Monetary Union gives
it access to the French guarantee of convertibility with the
French franc, which provides an additional margin of flexibility.
No precise balance of payments can be drawn up for Mauritania, as a good part of its commerce is unrecorded and takes
place over the virtually open borders in the south, the west,
and the north. In addition, transfers within the monetary union
are free and largely unrecorded. The diversion of imports to
Nouakchott from Dakar and the creation of SONIMEX have, of
course, increased the proportion of trade recorded by Mauritanian statistics. In February, 1970, the customs union with
Senegal was replaced with a trade agreement similar to those
with other UNDEAO countries. Most traditionally traded goods
will not be subject to duty, but Mauritania may tax all third-
country-origin goods imported through Senegal.
In the decade of the 1960's, a marked change took place
in the pattern of imports and exports, as well as in the trade
balance. Estimated foreign trade rose from some 60 per cent
of GDP in 1959 to some 80 per cent by the mid-1960's and there-
after. Exports rose from 20 per cent of GDP in 1959 to 46 per

THE ECONOMY OF MAURITANIA

TABLE 17

Estimated Foreign Trade, 1962, 1965, and 1968
(Billion CFAF)

Item	1962	1965	1968
Exports (f.o.b.)			
Recorded	0.98	14.28	18.18
Unrecorded	2.35	2.00	2.22
Total exports	3.33	16.28	20.40
Imports (c.i.f.)			
Recorded	8.81	6.14	9.34
Unrecorded	11.67	8.75	6.43
Total imports	20.48	14.89	15.77
Estimated trade balance	-17.15	1.39	4.63

Source: Data provided by Mauritanian authorities; cited
in Surveys of African Economies, Vol. III: Mauritania (Washington, D.C.: IMF, 1970), p. 386.

cent by 1968, while imports fell from 40 per cent of GDP to
35 per cent in the same period.

Mauritania's recorded trade statistics, based on customs
returns, can only give a partial picture of the volume and direction of imports and exports, since they are mainly based
on commodities passing through Nouakchott and Port-Etienne.
The recorded figures do not include those imports from Senegal
that are not declared as going to Mauritania when passed through
customs at Dakar. Aside from the problem of contraband and
coverage, the Customs Service failed in the past to send to
the Statistical Service all of the declarations of imports that
it received, a situation that is being improved. Further, importers may undervalue imports by an undetermined amount.

In exports, the principal feature has been the sharp rise
in the value of exports of iron ore, which are responsible for
almost all the rise in total exports from 1963 through 1967.
Most of this ore is exported to the United Kingdom and the
EEC. It is estimated that exports to areas outside the franc
zone account for about three-fourths of Mauritania's total exports. The figures do not include animals exported on the

hoof, mainly to Senegal. The annual value of these exports has been estimated at some CFAF 2 billion. (See Appendix Table 16.)

The volume of imports has fluctuated mainly with the rate of investment in large projects. These investments were high in 1962 and 1963, when MIFERMA was under construction and work was in progress on the new capital at Nouakchott. With a falling-off of such investment in 1964, imports of capital goods also declined sharply. In 1965, a further sharp rise in imports was recorded, although not to the highs previously attained, principally due to the building of the new wharf at Nouakchott, the fish-processing plants at Port-Etienne, and the refrigerator plant-abattoir at Kaedi.

By 1969, iron-ore exports accounted for the bulk of all exports. (See Appendix Table 17.) Fish exports rose rapidly after 1965, with an estimated value of CFAF 1.25 billion by 1969. The bulk of the rest of recorded exports consisted of gum arabic and hides and skins.

The sharp rise in the value of recorded imports in 1967 was due mainly to the expanded customs coverage resulting from the rerouting of trade to Nouakchott and Port-Etienne and the starting of SONIMEX operations. This company's imports in 1969 amounted to some CFAF 2.3 billion, an amount that would not have been recorded before 1967. Prior to 1967, imports for the public sector financed by foreign aid were not recorded. They were estimated to have declined by more than half between 1962 and 1967. By 1966 and 1969, the recorded import statistics started to show the impact of equipment imports for the construction of the copper mines at Akjoujt.

The main source of unrecorded imports is Senegal and consists of goods produced there and goods imported through Dakar and transshipped by road to Mauritania. The opening of the wharf at Nouakchott diverted a good part of this trade, but the volume of such unrecorded imports is still believed to be large. The economics of transportation in the southern region of Mauritania favor movement through Dakar for many imported goods, while the better developed Senegalese road system makes movement in that country faster and cheaper than on the other side of the river in Mauritania. In short, even where distances are comparable from points of importation, Senegalese shippers still have a significant advantage.

In 1967, unrecorded imports rose sharply because of fishing-boat imports by SOMAP. Fish from the Canary Islands fishing boats that land at Port-Etienne processing plants are also unrecorded. The Spanish Sahara has been a traditional source of contraband imports into Mauritania. Estimated imports from this source rose from CFAF 1 billion in 1962 to some CFAF 2.5 billion in 1969. A free zone was set up for Spanish Sahara goods in 1969, which enabled better estimates to be made of the total value of this trade.

The direction of trade has changed greatly in the 1960's. France supplied some 54 per cent of Mauritania's recorded imports in 1964 (down from 75 per cent in 1960) but accounted for only about 39 per cent by 1969, although its share would probably be higher if French unrecorded imports through Senegal were included. In this period, the share of the rest of the EEC in total imports rose slightly to about 14 per cent. The participation of the Western Hemisphere countries (mainly the United States) fell in relative terms but rose in value as the total value of trade rose sharply between 1964 and 1969.

On the export side, France declined from close to 100 per cent in 1962, when gum arabic was the main recorded export, to about 20 per cent in the period of 1964-1969, when iron ore was the principal export. By 1969, the United Kingdom was taking about 28 per cent of total exports in the form of iron ore, and the EEC, excluding France, about 42 per cent. African countries, particularly the People's Republic of Congo, was the main market for dried fish.

Trade is not entirely unrestricted, but the restrictions appear to have little effect in diverting its direction. Under the arrangements of the Associated West African Countries with the EEC, trade has been progressively liberalized so that only a few items, such as cars, are still subject to licensing, while all imports from the franc area are free. A quota system exists for imports from the rest of the world, but the limits are sufficiently wide so as to constitute no barrier. The monopoly of SONIMEX with respect to a number of basic consumer goods has been discussed earlier.

Discriminatory tariffs in favor of members of the UNDEAO and the EEC may be of greater importance in redirecting trade, particularly in such commodities as textiles. Since the great bulk of Mauritanian imports are capital goods financed with tied foreign aid from Europe or with capital supplied by private investors, usually on a duty-free basis, however, the effects of special quota and tariff arrangements could not have been great in influencing the over-all pattern of trade.

THE BALANCE OF PAYMENTS

The construction of an accurate balance of payments for Mauritania is difficult. Available data largely covers transactions only with countries outside the franc area. As has been shown, even trade data must be estimated to a large extent, and the country's foreign liabilities and assets are difficult to estimate because the bank notes of one country of the West African Monetary Union circulate freely in the other countries. Bank notes constitute about 30 per cent of Mauritania's money supply. Nevertheless, estimates of sufficient reliability can be made from the national accounts and from information and estimates published by the International Monetary Fund (IMF) some of which is incorporated in the estimates used here.

From 1959 to 1964, a sharp rise in foreign trade took place, as imports of capital equipment and manufactured goods almost offset rising iron-ore exports. The growth of private-factor payments reflect interest payments for the investment in mining. Private remittances are the net balance between the transfers of salary income by foreigners and the inflow of pensions to Mauritanian nationals by France.

Capital inflows almost offset the current account deficit in 1964. To the extent that imports consist of private capital imports for new mining or fishing-industry investments, there will be a corresponding private-capital inflow. Public-capital inflows consist of various forms of foreign aid loans, mainly from France in 1959 and 1964. Private-capital inflows for the MIFERMA mines are also connected with the factor payments to MIFERMA on past investments. This occurs because the further development of the mines requires reinvestment of earnings to a certain extent.

The figures for the three years given in Table 18 show a more even development of the main balance of payments parameters than, in fact, occurred. Between 1964 and 1968, the trade balance became quite favorable. Official capital flows were also at high and rising levels in these years. Factor payments on private investments and private transfers more than offset capital inflows, however. Large private-capital inflows occurred in 1967, when suppliers' credits were used to finance fishing boats, and, in 1969, there were large reported imports of machinery and equipment for the new copper mines. Provisional figures for 1969 show both imports and private capital rising by CFAF 3.5 billion. Thus, in both 1967 and 1969, private-capital inflow exceeded private-capital outflow.

TABLE 18

Estimated Balance of Payments, 1959, 1964, and 1968
(Billions CFAF francs)

	1959	1964	1968
Exports, (f.o.b.)	3.3	13.8	20.4
Imports, (c.i.f.)	6.9	13.7	15.8
	-3.6	+.1	+4.6
Nonfactor services, (net)	+2.3	-.6	-2.1
	-1.3	-.5	+2.5
Other unidentified	+.4	+1.3	-1.9
	-.9	+.8	+.6
Factor payments & private remittances	-0.7	-5.3	-8.1
Total current	-1.6	-4.5	-7.5
Public capital (net)	2.3	2.6	3.4
Private capital (net)	-.7	1.5	3.1
Total capital	1.6	4.1	6.5
Net monetary movements	n.a.	-.4	-1.0

Source: Surveys of African Economies, Vol. III: Mauritania (Washington, D.C.: IMF, 1970), pp. 394-400, for the IMF's estimated balance of payments.

The other unidentified account is included in the current account in these estimates. Since 1964, it has risen consistently and reportedly reached CFAF 4.4 billion in 1969, bigger than the entire capital inflow. It is believed that these large figures are mainly associated with private-sector transfers of profits and capital. Mauritania's deficit on services is also increasing. This item includes the Mauritanian cost of technical assistance and payments by mining companies for transportation, insurance, and other services.

Public-capital inflows include, in the second part of the 1960's, a mixture of foreign loans from the Caisse Centrale, FAC, the French Treasury, and IDA. There was also a drawdown of Caisse Centrale loans by the BMD and semipublic agencies. Grants from abroad averaged about CFAF 2.4 billion annually in the second part of the 1960's. The counterpart to these grants usually appears as imports for the projects being financed or as services connected with the aid program. (See Appendix Table 19.) During the second part of the 1960's, Mauritania's net foreign assets declined by some CFAF 3 billion.

FOREIGN AID AND INVESTMENT

The major foreign resource development variables in Mauritania may be defined as, first, the amount of resources that the country can spend productively and, second, the amount that it can acquire on suitable terms. The preceding chapters have given some insight into the absorptive capacity of the country. The amounts that Mauritania has been able to acquire since independence will be covered here. Clearly, the form of foreign aid, whether grant or loan, will also be important in gauging the real resources that are available for further development.

Further, foreign investment and technical assistance constitute a critical element in developing Mauritania's natural resources and, hence, its productive capacity. At the same time, such investment provides the bulk of the investment resources required, although a substantial part of it is repatriated under the terms of the concessions granted, which, in addition, usually fail to provide for substantial indirect benefits to the economy.

Mauritania receives public international assistance in grant form from the French Government through FAC, from the EEC through FED, from the United Nations in the form of technical assistance, and from the U.S. Government in the form of some food supplies related to a small Peace Corps program for local development projects. French aid through FAC covers the local and foreign financing of development projects agreed to by the two governments. It also covers direct budget subsidies, described in more detail under the budget, and the foreign cost, including salaries, of a large technical assistance program involving some 250 advisers, technicians, teachers, and officials. Mauritania provides local housing for these officials, as well as a living allowance of some CFAF 30,000 a month per person.

From 1960 through 1964, the financing of public development expenditures with foreign aid, including grants and concessional loans, amounted to CFAF 10.6 billion. Of this, CFAF 8.8 billion were in the form of FAC subsidies to the budget and project aid outside the budget. The balance of CFAF 1.8 billion was in the form of FED aid for projects. From 1965 through 1969, (estimated) total foreign aid amounted to CFAF 12.1 billion, of which some CFAF 5.7 billion were in the form of FAC aid. French aid declined from 83 per cent to 49 per cent of the total between the two periods. (See Appendix Table 13.)

FED aid rose from some 16 per cent to close to 40 per cent in this period. The IBRD group aid became significant in 1969 when it amounted to an estimated 18 per cent of the total. These figures leave out the value of technical assistance aid, mainly from France, which amounted to some CFAF 2.3 billion from 1960 to 1964 and to an estimated CFAF 2.9 billion from 1965 to 1969. Total foreign aid showed a tendency to rise from a low of CFAF 1.7 billion in 1965 to an estimated CFAF 2.9 billion annually in the years 1967, 1968, and 1969, a total reached earlier only in 1963.

The terms of aid also changed significantly during the decade. In the first five years, grant aid, excluding technical assistance, amounted to some 83 per cent of the total. In 1968, concessional loans amounted to 30 per cent of the total and, in 1969, to 45 per cent of the total. In addition, in 1969, an estimated additional CFAF 1.1 billion in suppliers' credits were received. Commitments by foreign aid and financing agencies, of course, are different from disbursements.

Normally, in a situation where total aid is expanding, commitments can be expected to exceed disbursements greatly in any given year. In general, the terms of aid to Mauritania are hardening as the relative importance of FAC and FED grant programs decline. Nevertheless, foreign financing still constitutes the only important and relatively stable source of development resources available to Mauritania.

Mauritania's external disbursed public debt rose from $21.6 million in 1967 to some $30 million by 1969. Conventionally, the burden of this debt is measured as a per cent of export earnings. In 1967, this ratio was about 1 per cent and, in 1969, was estimated at 2.3 per cent. In view of the absence of a real foreign exchange constraint in Mauritania, a more relevant way of measuring the impact of rising external indebtedness is in terms of domestic public finances. From 1960 to 1968, central government budget public debt payments rose from 2.3 per cent of total current outlays to 8.8 per cent.

Since the central government budget constitutes only part of the public sector, the real claim on public savings is the total payments on the external public debt. In 1969, identifiable interest and amortization payments on the external public debt amounted to an estimated $2.9 million, or some CFAF 800 million.* The total public-sector debt service amounted to some 20 per cent of total foreign aid and suppliers' credits received by Mauritania in that year.**

An important source of finance for the public and private sector has been the Caisse Centrale de Coopération Economique, a French public agency that provides loans and equity financing in accordance with French Government development policy. (In Appendix Table 20, a breakdown is given of Caisse Centrale loan disbursements from 1962 through 1969 to the central government, semipublic agencies, private firms, and others. In Appendix Table 21, the total outstanding financial commitments of the Caisse Centrale in Mauritania are listed from 1961 through 1967, including its equity position.) A substantial portion of Caisse Centrale operations in Mauritania has concerned loans and equity participation in fishing enterprises, a good proportion of which has not worked out.

In the private sector, as has been shown, substantial investments from private sources took place in the fishing and mining sector. The MIFERMA mines alone are estimated to have required an investment of over $200 million, of which $66 million were in the form of IBRD loans made in 1959, some $53.5 million of which were still outstanding by the end of 1968.

---

*The largest debt, for which no details are available, is some $3.6 million owed to the Chinese People's Republic, which was spent on the rice project in the delta.

**See Appendix Table 22 for a partial listing of outstanding central government debt and service payments in 1969.

The Akjoujt project is expected to require some $60 million in new investment, for which the financing plan calls for $4.5 million from the Mauritanian Government, which, in turn, will acquire this from the Caisse Centrale and FAC. The IFC and the EIB have agreed to lend $31 million for the project, and the IFC will take 15 per cent of the equity ($1.2 million); the balance will come from private foreign sources.

Mauritania received some $100 per capita in foreign grant aid and concessional loans from abroad, including technical assistance, in the period from 1960 to 1968.* If the IBRD group loans to private mines are included in this, another $70 per capita in foreign aid would have to be added, although these loans are on more conventional terms. An additional $30 per capita would have to be added if Caisse Centrale loans to the private sector are included. In the period 1959 through 1968, GDP per capita rose from some $65 to about $145 at current prices. As has been seen, the bulk of this rise was concentrated among relatively modern-sector wage and salary earners associated with mining, fishing, and the government sectors and related service activities in the northeastern part of the country.

---

*At the post-August 10, 1969, exchange rate of CFAF 277.71 = $1.00.

PART

CONCLUSIONS

11

REFLECTIONS ON
DEVELOPMENT STRATEGY
AND
DEVELOPMENT LESSONS

The economy of Mauritania is intensively dual in character. The traditional rural economy was little affected by the sharp changes that occurred in the northeast as a result of the introduction of the MIFERMA iron mines, a fish-processing industry at Port-Etienne, and the creation of the new administrative capital at Nouakchott. It is estimated that the modern sector employs less that 5 per cent of the labor force, while a considerable part of the wages paid go to expatriates, who predominate in the middle- and higher-paid positions.

In aggregate national income terms, the growth of the economy has been nothing short of spectacular, even when figures are reduced to an average per capita basis. These figures are, however, relatively meaningless when account is taken of the wide disparity in income distribution between the modern and traditional sectors; average GDP per capita in the modern sector may be roughly estimated at ten times that of the traditional sector.

Originally seen as the key to the country's economic development, MIFERMA has not earned sufficient profits to enable it to pay income taxes in the amounts anticipated. Output at over 8 million tons annually is well above earlier projections. The company provides directly over 25 per cent of current government revenues through royalties and taxes and more if direct and indirect taxes on its employees are included. MIFERMA has been and is a major factor in providing budgeting resources and modern sector employment; government spending in support of public services is probably also relatively high. It is not however, expected to increase greatly its

contribution to government finances or the GDP in the fore-
seeable future and a renegotiation of the long term tax scheme
may be in order if major new ore deposits prove to be com-
mercially interesting. A further major expansion may be expected in the modern sector as the Akjoujt copper mines come
into full operation, although no significant returns to the budget are expected until the mid-1970's.

The first attempt at modern planning was the four-year
plan, which started in mid-1963. By the end of 1966, it was
abandoned, and 1967-70 became a period of reassessment and
preparation for the new plan, which began in 1970. The IBRD
technical assistance mission was sent to Mauritania at the request of the government in spring, 1967, and produced suggested guidelines for a four-year program of development. These
guidelines were in large part accepted by the government and
constitute the basis for the new plan.

The major objectives of the first plan were to reduce the
dependence of the country on foreign financing and personnel
and to prepare the basis for the next stage of development
through a program of infrastructure investments and basic
studies. Neither of these objectives were by and large achieved.
The French subsidy to the current budget was relinquished by
Mauritania in 1963, and the government decided to adopt a
fiscal policy of severe austerity in order to husband scarce resources. Although fiscal stability was maintained, current outlays for essential maintenance and development services were
inadequate. Despite this effort large French subsidies were
needed to balance expenditures in the capital budget that could
not be financed under the foreign-financed development program
or through the current budget. Because of the scarcity of trained
personnel, the numbers of foreigners in Mauritania in bilateral
and multilateral technical assistance programs has remained
approximately constant.

The new strategy being pursued implies a fairly basic
change in development planning from the 1963-67 plan. In the
past, particularly before and during the first plan, the primary
emphasis of development strategy and of resource allocation
was given to creating the economic infrastructure and carrying
out the basic studies that were to become the foundation for a
later period of economic and social development. A good deal
was done in the way of establishing the administrative apparatus
of the new government, including the establishment of a new
capital at Nouakchott and a wharf that enabled commerce to
be redirected from Dakar.

Much, however, in the way of public resources was ex-
pended for poorly conceived and ill-coordinated projects. By

the end of the first plan, it was clear that, despite the high
hopes attached to the dramatic growth of the modern sector,
the basic problem of raising the standard of living of the bulk
of the population was not being solved. Although a great deal
of money had been spent on highly capital-intensive and relatively small hydroagricultural works, the results obtained did
not in retrospect, in most cases, warrant the investments
made. Too little emphasis had been placed on returns from
investments that affected the bulk of the rural population.

In part, the planners did not know enough about the ecological possibilities of traditional livestock and crop agriculture
and, in part, they placed excessive reliance on the stimulative
effects of infrastructure investments. In addition, the basic
studies that must be the foundation of any long-term effort to
transform the economic and social structure have yet, in most
cases, to be accomplished.

In short, the country seemed to be in a vicious economic
circle. Output was too small to justify or provide the resources for major infrastructure investments. Accordingly, incomes
of the bulk of the population were low, and government revenues,
despite revenues from mining, were inadequate to finance a
major expansion in public health and education. Public investments, largely financed with French and EEC aid, were not
having the desired effect of changing the structure of production
of the rural population.

The new strategy proposes a program of substantially
raising livestock and crop output by improving present methods
of herding and cultivation. In part, it is based on successes
obtained in the past by limited investments in animal sanitation,
rural well-digging, and experiments with millet and sorghum
output, and, in part, it relies on the concentration of extension
workers, together with the introduction of simple changes in
technology in selected areas to achieve significant results in
the next few years. Successes in these selected areas would
then be the model for introducing similar changes throughout
the rural economy. A good deal of attention will have to be
given to improving the credit, storage, and distribution system
for grain if the program to raise output is to succeed.

Although selected hydroagricultural works are recommended, these and the studies required to bring them to the stage of
implementation should be intended to contribute mainly to development in future plan periods and to constitute a logical
complementary step as output levels of the bulk of the rural
population rise close to the limits that relatively inexpensive
changes in production techniques and organization can produce.

The lessons learned with the irrigation experiments of the past few years can provide valuable guides for future project planners. No extension of relatively high-cost livestock-processing facilities is recommended in the near future.

The proposed program is based on a determination of the technological possibilities in both the livestock and crop agricultural sectors and takes into consideration the problems of furnishing adequate capital, trained manpower, and supporting government services. In accordance with this strategy, the highest-priority projects should be those with the lowest ratios of invested capital to output; these usually also affect the largest number of producers.

A development program for Mauritania should be highly operational within the context of a four-year period, for it should be based on individual projects in selected areas, with as careful an evaluation as present data will permit of required inputs and projected outputs. Considerable preparation will be required before individual projects can be undertaken. The program should have the effect of meeting the basic food needs of the population, raising per capita standards of living of the bulk of the rural population, leading to a progressive monetization of trade, and improving the basic structure of Mauritania's balance of payments. In contrast to alternatives considered, it should not rely upon the uncertain process of spreading the benefits from a few highly capital-intensive projects in order to raise rural income levels. It also should not involve placing the kind of burden on the social structure and the administrative and educational system that the introduction of a more complex technology would require.

Foreign financing agencies, in the past, became impatient with the large number of individual requests for financing that came from Mauritanian sources, many of which were poorly evaluated from a technical and economic point of view and most of which had no clear relation to a coordinated program of development. To obtain the necessary finance for a program of development, it was recognized that the program itself must be the basis for requests for financing. This required the creation of sectoral programs within which projects are ranked by priority, as well as a national plan to coordinate the sectoral programs with government economic policy and available foreign aid. A good deal of progress was made with sectoral programming after the first plan, particularly in livestock and agriculture.

One of the critical constraints to the achievement of development objectives, regardless of which strategy and program are adopted, is the absence in Mauritania of a government administrative apparatus capable of directing such an effort. For this reason, the government established a planning appa- ratus to integrate the function of over-all plan and policy formu- lation and execution with the process of preparing and carrying out sectoral programs and their related projects.

The reform adopted is the minimum necessary to make the proposed development program operational. It takes ac- count of the problem of shortages of trained personnel and the financial limitations to which the government is subject. As experience is gained and as more trained people and resources become available for the development effort, additional and more far-reaching reforms in public administration will be appropriate.

Specifically, the plan organization was reorganized and made into an independent ministry that also controls the critical rural sector. Ideally, it is to coordinate the activities of programers within the operating ministries, although, in practice, lack of trained personnel has made this difficult. A mechanism has been proposed to advise the Cabinet on eco- nomic and development policy issues. An annual development plan is being drawn up each year and coordinated with the bud- get in order to make the development plan operational. The budget itself will have to be reorganized to make it develop- ment oriented and usable as an instrument of economic policy- making.

The new development plan for the period 1970-73 appears to come close to meeting these criteria and constraints. It is a pragmatic document that proposes a list of projects ar- ranged by sectors, most of which are consistent with the rural-based strategy of development. It recognizes the need for careful study of project costs and benefits, for having an adequate cadre of personnel to plan and carry out projects, and for providing for the inevitable recurrent costs associated with fixed investments.

It is not, in fact, a plan in the conventional sense, for it contains no macroeconomic framework that promises meaning- less average annual growth rates. Rather, it is a collection of things to do that can be considered, in the light of national priorities, as part of an annual exercise in programing budg- etary resources and available foreign aid. It augurs well for the future development of the country, for it places great stress on basic studies, as well as on project preparation. Finally, it recognizes the critical role that trained human re- sources must play in widening development opportunities.

Mauritania is fortunate in being able to rely on large numbers of foreign technicians, as well as large amounts of grant
aid. The development program under consideration would not,
in the short run, lessen this dependence. Rather, in plan administration, sectoral programing, and project evaluation,
it would be only realistic to recognize that more, rather than
fewer, foreign experts are required. In general, the government would do well to regard technical assistance, as well as
foreign-financed aid, as a scarce resource, the use of which
should be optimized in the interests of development. Until
Mauritanians can be trained in adequate numbers to fill the
numerous positions requiring skilled personnel, the availability of large numbers of French and U.N. technical assist-
ants can be a vital supplement to the few Mauritanians capable
of participating at the higher levels of modern government
administration.

Mauritania's development is not entirely unique. Other
countries have experienced the problems of modern-sector
enclaves, which create, in effect, dual economies. Other
countries, particularly in the same geographic zone, have
similar types of resource constraints and large nomadic
populations governed by relatively new administrative systems.
All have the problems of fostering a national consciousness
while responding to what they perceive as economic and social
development objectives. There are some lessons in the Mauritanian experience with nation-building and development worth
identifying that may have a wider applicability.

The major lessons stem from the confrontation of a
dynamic Western culture with an Arabic Moorish culture rich
in its own traditions and customs. Although the Western world
has succeeded, in the past, in imposing its political will on
the Moor and, in recent times, its technology and entrepreneur-
ship, it has not succeeded in destroying the fabric of Moorish
society and the values that sustain it. There can be no dispute
that substantial inroads have been made by the West and that
educated Moors and government officials move with almost
equal ease in Paris as in Nouakchott. Yet, the country has
not become overwhelmed by what is termed the "revolution of
rising expectations" that would lead to the rapid abandonment
of existing ways for the illusion of a better immediate life in
the modern sector.

Mauritanian leaders have understood the limitations of
modern-sector enclaves for producing a rapid economic and
social transformation of their people. In the future, one would
expect that they will try to extract the maximum in benefits

from those islands of modernity and any new concessionaires. They will attempt to improve the links between the enclaves and the rest of the economy. Yet, the vast reaches of the country and the fact that modern-sector activity is in the least populated part of the country make it unlikely that close links can be forged between the rural herdsmen and peasants and the technocrats in the mines, processing plants, and offices.

Accordingly, the basic strategy adopted of developing the rural sector is one most likely to permit the gradual evolution of traditional ways in step with the economic potential of livestock-herding and peasant agriculture. Mauritania is fortunate in having unexploited margins for expanding output on its grasslands and for increasing returns from peasant agriculture while population pressures are comparatively low. By concentrating development efforts in the rural sectors, a significant rise in the well-being of the bulk of the country's inhabitants should be possible.

In this process, the resources can be acquired from the incremental growth of per capita incomes to provide for future development opportunities, as well as to anticipate the demographic consequences of the general introduction of modern medicine and sanitation. These future opportunities will have to be based on higher-productivity activities and will involve more sophisticated techniques in both the livestock and agricultural sectors. They will bring with them demands for related services. When the time comes, the country will be better prepared in human- and material-resource terms and in terms of institutions to absorb the changes in technology and ways of living that development will bring.

It would be easy to be misunderstood in drawing this kind of lesson from the circumstances and experience of a country as poor and relatively untouched as Mauritania. There can be little dispute with the facts concerning the social conditions of much of the country's inhabitants, who have little or no access to modern medical care, education, housing, and opportunity. Yet, it is also true, that this human condition has existed since prehistoric times in the sub-Sahara. It is really a matter of alternatives. Would the people of Mauritania be better off if the great mass of them had migrated to the towns and demanded services and jobs that could not be provided?

Already, the rapid growth of the main towns has caused shortages in basic public services requiring large public investments, which, to some extent, will take place at the expense of infrastructure works that could have wider productivity as well as distributional impacts. Mauritania, of course, has

no large cities by outside standards, and there is a case for
developing concentrated markets, which will allow minimum-
scale levels of manufacturing plants to be reached and other
economic and social activities to grow.

   Urbanization is also a necessary process in the transformation from traditional to modern types of activity. In
particular, the interior towns could well be regarded as centers
where processing, services, administrative functions, and
cultural activities could be organized in support of the growing
livestock and peasant agriculture activities. To encourage
actively a rate of urbanization that would overwhelm the country's administrative apparatus and absorb its limited resources,
however, would hardly constitute a service to the people, who
are the object of development. The fact is that the supply of
labor is virtually infinitely elastic with respect to the modern
sector, and words like unemployment and underemployment
do not mean a great deal in terms of the real policy and resource options open to a country like Mauritania.

   Another lesson that is important in the above concerns
what might well be termed the illusion of the benefits of
foreign aid and related technology. Mauritania, as has been
shown, is highly dependent on foreign grants and loans to finance
its development, both public and private. In the past, it relied
too heavily on strategies that derived from the conditioning and
experience of Western technocrats in terms of giving advice
and financing works that paid too little attention to the possibilities and needs of Mauritania. Specific examples have been
cited such as an expensive experimental water and electricity
desalinization plant that cost relatively little in capital but will
produce high-cost water and electricity. Further, an airplane
that costs more to operate than it can earn in revenues must
at best be a questionable gift.

   On a larger scale, it has been seen how poor planning and
management of a major fish-processing industry has led to
serious losses on the part of Mauritania and the foreign public
agencies associated with it and has caused a retardation in the
development of one of the country's most promising resources.
National expectations of the benefits from the large foreign-
financed iron mines were not met. The siren call of modern
technology allowed the engineers to build enormously expensive
and largely unremunerative irrigation works in the Senegal
River basin and, in the process, to use up a good deal of foreign
aid.

   Even worse, such works could have no more than a marginal impact on the local peasant, who had neither the capital nor

the training to learn from these projects and found little employment in them. Not all foreign aid, then, is a blessing.
It seems that the Mauritanians have come to realize that only
by determining and controlling their own strategy of development can they hope to acquire and use foreign aid of the type
and in amounts sufficient to create real development.

Foreign aid agencies genuinely concerned with the effective
use of aid should find increasing opportunities to expand their
operations in Mauritania. The aid given will have to be largely
on soft terms, given the domestic financial constraints that
have been discussed. It will also have to be aid that will take
real effort and involvement. Although some capital-intensive
foreign-engineered and -supplied "turnkey" projects will still
be needed, development will increasingly have to concern
"hard-core" projects in traditional livestock-herding and
peasant agriculture.

Allocation of Investments of Four-Year Plan, 1963-66

Nature of Investments	Amount of Investments (million CFAF)	Per Cent of Public Investments	Per Cent of Private Investments	Per Cent of Total Plan Investments
General studies				
Public	580. 8	4. 3	-	5. 7
Private	1, 000. 0	-	7. 0	
Transport & communications infrastructure				
Public	3, 191. 0	23. 5	-	12. 1
Private	160. 0	-	1. 1	
Agriculture & Livestock				
Public	2, 352. 0	17. 4	-	8. 6
Private	48. 0	-	0. 3	
Mining production				
Public	800. 0	5. 9	-	33. 8
Private	8, 580. 0	-	60. 5	
Fishing industry				
Public	960. 0	7. 1	-	6. 9
Private	950. 0	-	6. 7	
Services & commerce				
Public	-	0. 0	-	4. 6
Private	1, 270. 0	-	9. 0	
Education & training				
Public	922. 5	6. 7	-	3. 3
Private	-	-	0. 0	
Health & hygiene				
Public	770. 4	5. 7	-	2. 8
Private	-	-	0. 0	
Urban Infrastructure & Housing				
Public	3, 043. 0	22. 4	-	14. 5
Private	980. 0	-	6. 9	
Administrative Buildings				
Public	947. 0	7. 0	-	7. 7
Private	1, 200. 0	-	8. 5	
Total				
Public	13, 566. 7	100. 0	-	100. 0
Private	14, 188. 0	-	100. 0	

Note: Plan provisions for public transport and communications infrastructure differ by CFAF 3 millions and public education and training by CFAF 1/2 million from text Table 2. The differences result from unexplained changes between the 1963 plan document and the bilan published in 1967.

Source: RIM, Plan Quadriennel de Développement Economique et Social, 1963-1966 (Nouakchott, 1963).

APPENDIX TABLE 2

Public Sector: Plan Investment Projections and Outcome,
July 1, 1963-June 30, 1967, by Category

Nature of Investment	Plan Provisions	Disburse- ments	Commit- ments	Per Cent of Plan Provisions*
	(million CFAF)			
General studies	581	366	475	63.0
Transport & communications infrastructure	3,188	2,376	4,038	74.5
Agriculture & livestock	2,352	1,176	1,758	50.0
Mining	800	262	262	32.8
Fishing	960	970	1,630	101.0
Education & training	922	393	869	42.6
Health & hygiene	770	804	932	104.4
Urban infrastructure & housing	3,043	1,072	2,924	35.2
Administrative buildings	947	525	989	55.4
Services	-	334	342	-
Total	13,563	8,278	14,219	61.0

*Disbursements divided by plan provisions.
Note: Plan provisions for public transport and communications infrastructure differ
by CFAF 3 millions and public education and training by CFAF 1/2 million from text
Table 1. The differences result from unexplained changes between the 1963 plan document
and the bilan published in 1967.

Source: RIM, Bilan d'Exécution Plan Quadriennal, 1963-66 (Nouakchott, 1967).

APPENDIX TABLE 3

Private Sector: Plan Investment Projections and Outcome,
July 1, 1963–June 30, 1967, by Category

Nature of Investment	Plan Provisions	Disburse-ments	Commit-ments	Per Cent of Plan Provisions*
	(million CFAF)			
General studies	1,000	214	389	21.4
Transport & communi-cations infrastructure	160	–	–	–
Agriculture & livestock	48	107	107	222.9
Mining	8,580	11,293	11,293	131.6
Fishing	950	13,110	4,121	327.4
Urban infrastructure & housing	980	1,290	1,240	131.6
Administrative buildings	1,200	650	650	54.2
Services	1,270	1,765	1,765	139.2
Total	14,188	18,429	19,615	129.9

*Disbursements divided by plan provisions.

Source: RIM, Bilan d'Exécution Plan Quadriennal, 1963–66 (Nouakchott, 1967).

APPENDIX TABLE 4

Average Per Capita Monthly Wages in the
Modern Private Sector, 1962-70
(Thousand CFAF)

Activity	1962	1963	1965	1967	1970*
Agriculture & fishing	17. 5	18	22	22	25
Mining	45. 0	46	55	55	63
Processing industry	20. 0	18	27	25	29
Building & public works	24. 0	20	26	25	29
Water & electricity	26. 0	28	27	36	41
Commerce & banking	25. 0	35	37	42	48
Transport	30. 0	27	27	28	32
Other services	12. 0	19	21	15	19
Average	27. 5	32	40	40	46

*Estimated.

Sources: RIM, Bulletin Statistique et Economique, No. 8 (1965); and RIM, Ministère de la Planification et du Développement Rural, Annuaire Statistique (Nouakchott, 1968).

APPENDIX TABLE 5

Employment of Mauritanians and Non-Mauritanians
in the Modern Private Sector, by Occupational Category, 1963-67

Breakdown	Management	Supervisors	Skilled Employees	Skilled Workers	Apprentices	Unskilled Workers	Total
1963							
Mauritanians	3	54	200	865	1,339	2,732	5,193
Non-Mauritanians	187	911	309	1,056	370	64	2,897
Total	190	965	509	1,921	1,709	2,796	8,090
Per cent of Mauritanians	2	6	40	45	79	98	65
1964							
Mauritanians	12	57	242	1,110	1,470	3,063	5,954
Non-Mauritanians	184	888	295	1,117	406	128	3,018
Total	196	945	537	2,227	1,876	3,191	8,972
Per cent of Mauritanians	6	6	45	50	78	96	67
1965							
Mauritanians	31	102	290	986	1,267	2,587	5,263
Non-Mauritanians	211	958	261	672	279	74	2,455
Total	242	1,060	551	1,658	1,546	2,661	7,718
Per cent of Mauritanians	13	10	53	60	82	97	68
1966							
Mauritanians	14	135	357	1,251	1,867	2,294	5,918
Non-Mauritanians	201	1,000	327	597	206	39	2,370
Total	215	1,135	684	1,848	2,073	2,333	8,288
Per cent of Mauritanians	7	12	52	68	90	98	71
1967							
Mauritanians	27	212	371	1,439	1,613	2,748	6,410
Non-Mauritanians	290	993	308	633	114	115	2,453
Total	317	1,205	679	2,072	1,727	2,863	8,863
Per cent of Mauritanians	9	17	53	70	93	96	72

Sources: RIM, Ministère de la Planification et du Développement Rural, Annuaire Statistique (Nouakchott, 1968); and Surveys of African Economies, Vol. III: Mauritania (Washington, D.C.: IMF, 1970), p. 348.

APPENDIX TABLE 6

Proportion of Foreigners in Modern
Private-Sector Employment, 1962 and 1965
(Per Cent)

Activity	1962	1965
Agriculture & fishing	14	15
Mining	36	32
Processing industry	65	55
Building & public works	35	31
Water & electricity	37	27
Commerce & banking	53	47
Transport	47	26
Other services	42	35
Total	39	32

Source: RIM, Situation de l'Emploi Salarié au 30 Novembre 1965 (June, 1966).

APPENDIX TABLE 7

Modern Private-Sector Employment, 1957-67*

Activity	1957 Number	1957 Per Cent of Total	1962 Number	1962 Per Cent of Total	1963 Number	1963 Per Cent of Total	1964 Number	1964 Per Cent of Total	1965 Number	1965 Per Cent of Total	1966 Number	1966 Per Cent of Total	1967 Number	1967 Per Cent of Total
Agriculture & fishing	30	8.7	337	2.9	326	4	400	4.4	470	6	489	6	583	6.6
Mining	217	14.6	2,287	19.4	3,265	40	3,515	39.2	3,881	50	4,075	50	4,178	47.5
Processing industry	16	1.3	153	1.4	191	3	273	3.0	138	2	153	2	107	1.2
Building & public works	594	40.0	6,775	57.6	2,503	30	2,653	29.5	1,435	19	1,831	20	2,042	23.1
Water & electricity	-	-	77	0.7	124	1	102	1.2	119	2	127	2	306	3.5
Commerce & banking	200	13.5	342	2.9	435	6	490	5.4	324	4	388	5	394	4.5
Transport	203	13.5	897	7.6	841	11	953	10.7	655	8	649	8	638	7.2
Other services	125	8.4	375	7.5	405	5	586	6.6	696	9	576	7	567	6.4
Total	1,385	100.0	11,243	100.0	8,090	100	8,972	100.0	7,718	100	8,288	100	8,815	100

*Figures do not correspond with those of Table   , as those are based on a census that omitted independent and irregular workers, as well as employees of a number of small establishments. In 1962, this resulted in an underestimate in the above number of some 500 service workers and, in 1965, of an estimated 300. The effects of these omissions on gross wage and salary estimates are negligible.

Sources: RIM, Situation de l'Emploi Salarié au 30 Novembre 1965 (June, 1966); and RIM, Bulletin Statistique et Economique (1968).

APPENDIX TABLE 8[*]

Livestock and Milk Products Consumed
Locally and Exported, 1968
(Million CFAF)

Product	Domestic Consumption		Exports	
	Self Consump-tion	Marketed	Official	Total
Livestock				
Cattle	140	490	270	1,050
Sheep & goats	520	715	100	900
Camels	150	525	25	330
Asses	-	-	-	20
Total	810	1,730	395	2,300
Milk	7,900	700	-	-

[*]Producer prices.

Source: RIM, Ministère de la Planification et du Développement Rural, Comptes Economiques de la République Islamique de Mauritanie (1968).

APPENDIX TABLE 9

Principal Rural-Sector Products Consumed Locally and Exported, 1959, 1964, and 1968*
(Million CFAF)

Product	Domestic Consumption			Exports		
	1959	1964	1968	1959	1964	1968
Self-Consumption						
Agriculture	1,565	1,650	1,670			
Livestock	800	800	810			
Dairying	4,400	5,775	7,900			
Fishing	100	200	180			
Total	6,865	8,425	10,560			
Marketed						
Agriculture	270	1,030	1,535	320	645	430
Livestock	800	1,500	2,115	2,940	2,990	2,800
Dairying	400	600	700	-	-	-
Fishing	260	300	490	53	365	1,220
Total	1,730	3,430	4,840	3,313	4,000	4,450
Grand total	8,595	11,855	15,400			

*Market Prices.

Source: RIM, Ministère de la Planification et du Développement Rural, Comptes Economiques de la République Islamique de Mauritanie (1968).

143

APPENDIX TABLE 10

Summary of Current Budget Expenditures, 1960-68

Item	1960 Amount (million CFAF)	1960 Per Cent	1962 Amount (million CFAF)	1962 Per Cent	1964 Amount (million CFAF)	1964 Per Cent	1966 Amount (million CFAF)	1966 Per Cent	1968 Amount (million CFAF)	1968 Per Cent
By Function										
General administration	583	19.2	1,018	23.5	932	22.7	900	20.5	914	17.6
Army and police	312	10.3	877	20.3	1,070	26.0	983	22.4	1,177	22.7
Education	435	14.3	583	13.4	675	16.4	739	16.8	971	18.7
Health	223	7.3	262	6.0	257	6.2	310	7.1	365	7.1
Rural development	196	6.5	182	4.2	206	5.0	195	4.4	224	4.3
Economic affairs & planning	34	1.1	23	0.5	18	0.4	30	0.7	43	0.8
Public works & maintenance	301	9.9	273	6.3	257	6.2	301	6.8	349	6.8
Contribution toward technical assistance	30	1.0	26	0.6	81	2.0	91	2.1	99	1.9
Public debt	71	2.3	238	5.5	220	5.4	398	9.1	457	8.8
Purchases	70	2.3	302	7.0	34	0.8	31	0.7	69	1.3
Miscellaneous, contributions, subsidies, refunds	783*	25.8	551	12.7	367	8.9	412	9.4	519	10.0
Total	3,038	100.0	4,335	100.0	4,117	100.0	4,390	100.0	5,187	100.0
By Type of Expenditure										
Salaries	1,479	48.6	2,086	48.2	2,355	57.2	2,498	56.9	2,882	55.7
Maintenance	169	5.6	102	2.4	82	2.0	106	2.4	93	1.8
Materials & supplies	967	31.8	1,359	31.4	1,048	25.5	944	21.5	1,191	23.0
Transfers	357	11.7	540	12.5	411	10.0	445	10.1	555	10.7
Public debt	71	2.3	238	5.5	220	5.3	397	9.0	457	8.8
Total	3,043	100.0	4,325	100.0	4,116	100.0	4,390	100.0	5,178	100.0

*Includes independence celebrations.

Source: RIM, Ministry of Finance, Comptes Définitifs.

APPENDIX TABLE 11

Government Current Budget Expenditures, 1960-68
(Million CFAF)

Item	1960	1961	1962	1963	1964	1965	1966	1967	1968
Parliament & presidency	171	214	307	285	188	168	168	177	185
Justice	77	83	98	99	102	98	94	97	95
Interior	254	295	241	248	222	222	214	222	178
Police	312	316	577	582	526	474	481	537	594
Army	-	22	300	409	544	522	502	541	583
Foreign affairs	-	125	148	232	188	170	180	220	159
Information & radio	17	24	61	68	67	70	69	82	95
Finance	52	62	148	152	160	164	169	185	187
General education	417	387	562	650	648	717	719	852	914
Technical education	18	23	21	22	27	23	20	32	57
Public health, labor, social affairs	223	225	262	247	257	256	310	358	365
Civil service administration	12	13	15	21	5	12	6	11	15
Rural development	196	157	182	179	206	193	195	232	224
Economic affairs & planning	34	18	23	19	18	29	30	33	43
Public works	133	179	171	185	176	162	195	237	256
Maintenance	168	93	102	107	81	109	106	134	93
Miscellaneous current expenditures	459	204	158	179	152	200	187	239	197
Contribution & subsidies	290	225	197	172	142	198	179	243	258
Contribution toward technical assistance	30	26	26	41	81	83	91	81	99
Public debt service	71	576	238	106	220	214	398	301	457
Purchases (cars, furniture, material)	70	99	302	73	34	30	31	50	69
Refunds	34	46	196	211	73	40	46	52	64
Total current expenditures	3,038	3,412	4,335	4,287	4,117	4,154	4,390	4,916	5,187
Loans to public enterprises & participation	-	108	39	10	20	4	-	3	-
Contribution toward construction of Nouakchott	23	188	17	31	-	-	-	-	-
Transfer to development budget	80	27	208	-	-	-	20	52	195
Total expenditures of current budget	3,141	3,735	4,599	4,328	4,137	4,158	4,410	4,971	5,382

Source: RIM, Ministry of Finance, Comptes Définitifs.

Government Current Budget Revenues, 1960-69
(Million CFAF)

Item	1960	1961	1962	1963	1964	1965	1966	1967	1968	1969
Direct Taxes										
Revenue taxes	143	351	661	585	821	963	828	843	954	1,102
Other direct taxes	121	217	247	230	64	63	89	78	87	146
Total	264	568	908	815	885	1,026	917	921	1,041	1,248
MIFERMA taxation	-	187	200	538	630	1,084	1,604	1,455	1,439	1,432
Indirect Taxes										
Import duties	542	1,064	1,124	1,076	1,102	1,078	932	1,031	920	846
Turnover tax	68	235	593	664	586	527*	622	710	749	825
Consumer taxes (tea, tobacco, sugar)	14	15	175*	15	6	245*	15	291*	673*	364*
Petroleum tax	23	58	84	95	152	177	180	209	265	358
Other internal taxes	6	86	21	28	46	129	105	109	126	59
Export taxes (other than iron ore)	4	5	8	8	8	34	49	48	53	70
Total	657	1,463	2,005	1,886	1,900	2,190	1,903	2,398	2,786	2,522
Registration and stamp taxes	23	31	52	70	52	84	85	102	97	119
Revenue from property, ports, and services	40	49	45	49	45	41	80	152	183	175
Central bank profits	-	-	-	-	97	68	68	90	106 }	333
Miscellaneous revenues	57	43	72	55	157	80	89	73	49 }	
Total current revenues	1,041	2,341	3,282	3,413	3,766	4,573	4,746	5,191	5,701	5,829
French current budget subsidies	1,483	1,821	1,852	500	-	-	-	-	-	-
Total revenues of current budget	2,524	4,162	5,134	3,913	3,766	4,573	4,746	5,191	5,701	5,829
Total current revenues (in per cent of GDP at factor costs)	5.3	10.4	14.4	14.8	11.9	12.4	12.2	12.8	13.3	13.3

*Includes contribution from sugar-price stabilization fund.

Source: RIM, Ministry of Finance, Comptes Définitifs.

146

APPENDIX TABLE 13

Public Development Expenditures and Their Financing, 1960-69
(Million CFAF)

Item	1960	1961	1962	1963	1964	1965	1966	1967	1968	1969*	Average 1960-64	Average 1965-69
EXPENDITURES												
Budgeted Expenditures												
Current budget	23	296	56	41	20	4	-	3	-	0	87	2
Equipment budget	281	146	653	524	428	291	772	686	538	663	406	572
Total	304	442	709	565	448	295	772	689	538	663	493	574
Nonbudgeted Foreign Aid												
Projects												
Grants	930	250	1,369	1,127	1,433	1,367	911	1,651	1,764	1,451	1,022	1,423
Loans & credits	100	850	136	1,384	128	48	285	564	1,032	1,444	520	482
Total	1,030	1,100	1,505	2,511	1,561	1,415	1,196	2,215	2,796	2,895	1,542	1,905
Investments financed with supplier credits	-	-	-	-	-	-	-	65	35	1,086	-	25
Total development expenditures	1,334	1,542	2,214	3,076	2,009	1,710	1,968	2,969	3,369	4,644	2,035	2,504
FINANCING OF DEVELOPMENT EXPENDITURES												
Foreign Aid												
French subsidies:												
Current budget	-	870	799	-	-	291	465	632	177	54	334	391
Equipment budget	20	-	402	401	428	-	-	-	-	-	250	-
French project aid outside two budgets	1,030	1,100	779	2,059	918	590	486	1,120	777	727	1,177	743
FED	-	-	715	439	628	756	563	842	1,269	988	356	858
IBRD/IDA	-	-	-	-	15	-	47	174	179	548	-	100
Other aid donors	-	-	11	13	-	69	100	79	571	632	8	205
Total	1,050	1,970	2,706	2,912	1,989	1,706	1,661	2,847	2,973	2,949	2,125	2,297
Supplier credits	-	-	-	-	-	-	-	65	35	1,086	-	25
Local Sources												
Current budget surpluses	-	-	-	-	-	419	356	277	564	0	-	404
Miscellaneous contributions	-	1	1	-	24	6	-	-	-	-	5	1
Total	-	1	1	-	24	425	356	277	564	0	5	405
Total financial resources	1,050	1,971	2,707	2,912	2,013	2,131	2,017	3,189	3,572	4,035	2,130	2,727
Impact on treasury reserves (- = increase)	284	-429	-493	164	-4	-421	-49	-220	-203	609	-95	-223

*Estimates.

Source: RIM, Ministry of Finance figures.

APPENDIX TABLE 14

Government Reserve Fund (Caisse de Reserve), 1960-69
(Million CFAF)

Item	1960	1961	1962	1963	1964	1965	1966	1967	1968	1969
Balance prior year	40.0	201.3	80.6	341.1	869.1	460.9	62.6	188.8	516.0	393.0
Surplus prior-year budget	342.6a	120.1b	426.8	528.0	21.8	.7	413.2	295.0	-	-
Total	382.6	321.4	507.4	869.1	890.9	461.6	475.8	483.8	-	-
Contribution to current budget	0.0	-240.8	0.0	0.0	-430.0	-400.0	0.0	-	-	-
Contribution to equipment budget	-181.3	0.0	-166.3c	0.0	0.0	+1.0	-287.0	-	-	-
Balance at end of year	201.3	80.6	341.1	869.1	460.9	62.6	188.8	516.0	393	201

aBelieved transferred from 1958.
bBelieved transferred from 1959.
cCovers 1962 and 1963.

Source: RIM, Treasury.

APPENDIX TABLE 15

Short-Term Credit, 1964-69
(Million CFAF, end of period)

Activity	1964	1965	1966	1967	1968	1969
Agriculture & livestock	-	-	-	-	-	12
Mining	70	326	-	100	117	113
Fisheries & other industrial activities	128	148	388	589	798	631
Construction & public works	77	136	99	280	746	427
Transport	83	92	179	274	307	648
Commerce	342	298	291	621	831	1,225
Other sectors or unclassified operations	166	136	67	236	667	1,069
Total credit from banking system	866	1,136	1,024	2,100	3,466	4,125

Source: IMF, International Financial Statistics.

149

APPENDIX TABLE 16

Estimated Foreign Trade, 1962-69
(Billion CFAF)

Item	1962	1963	1964	1965	1966	1967	1968	1969 (provisional)[a]
Exports (f.o.b.)								
Recorded	0.98	4.23	11.49	14.28	17.10	17.34	18.18	20.56
Unrecorded (livestock)	2.35	2.35	2.35	2.00	1.91	2.26	2.22	2.20
Total exports	3.33	6.58	13.84	16.28	19.01	19.60	20.40	22.76
Imports (c.i.f.)								
Recorded	8.81	7.42	3.88	6.14	5.68	9.10	9.34	11.70
Unrecorded								
Imports from Senegal	6.10	6.10	6.10	6.00	6.00	5.00	4.00	4.50
Imports of fishing boats	-	-	-	-	-	2.50	-	-
Purchases of fish from Canary Islands fishing fleet	0.17	0.17	0.29	0.35	0.40	0.56	0.43	0.62
Imports from Spanish Sahara	1.00	1.00	1.00	1.00	1.00	1.00	2.00	2.50
Foreign aid imports[b]	4.40	2.26	2.43	1.40	1.40	-	-	-
Total unrecorded imports	11.67	9.53	9.82	8.75	8.80	9.06	6.43	7.62
Total imports	20.48	16.95	13.70	14.89	14.48	18.16	15.77	19.32
Estimated trade balance	-17.15	-10.37	0.14	1.39	4.53	1.44	4.63	3.44

[a]In current CFAF; no adjustment made for devaluation of August 10, 1969.
[b]Since 1967, these imports have been included under recorded imports.

Source: Data provided by Mauritanian authorities; cited in Surveys of African Economies, Vol. III: Mauritania (Washington, D. C.: IMF, 1970), p. 386.

APPENDIX TABLE 17

Commodity Distribution of Recorded Foreign Trade, 1962-69
(Billion CFAF)

Item	1962	1963	1964	1965	1966	1967	1968	1969 [a]
Exports								
Iron ore	--	2.71	10.65	13.09	15.59	15.37	15.28	17.51
Fish	0.22	0.32	0.37	0.59	0.66	0.99	0.98	1.25
Gum arabic[b]	0.33	0.33	0.33	0.21	0.23	0.31	0.39	0.92
Other[c]	0.43	0.87	0.14	0.39	0.62	0.67	1.53	0.88[d]
Total recorded exports	0.98	4.23	11.49	14.28	17.10	17.34	18.18	20.56[d]
Imports								
Foodstuffs	0.43	0.26	0.27	0.49	0.77	1.50	2.17	--
Petroleum products	0.23	0.21	0.26	0.28	0.32	0.33	0.64	--
Vehicles & spare parts	0.40	0.92	0.41	1.04	0.60	0.56	0.66	--
Capital goods	6.14	3.31	1.50	2.28	2.05	3.82	2.86	--
Other	1.61	2.72	1.44	2.05	1.94	2.89	3.01	--[d]
Total recorded imports	8.81	7.42	3.88	6.14	5.68	9.10	9.34	11.70[d]

[a] In current CFAF; no adjustment made for devaluation of August 10, 1969.
[b] Adjusted to include the difference between total recorded production, all of which is exported, and exports as recorded by customs.
[c] Beginning in 1966, this item excludes value of re-exports of goods imported on a temporary basis. These do not appear in trade statistics at time of import, but are recorded when exported.
[d] Provisionale.

Sources: Comité Monetaire de la Zone Franc, La Zone Franc (1965); and Ministère de la Planifi-cation et du Développement Rural, Annuaire Statistique (Nouakchott, 1968); cited in Surveys of African Economies, Vol. III: Mauritania (Washington, D.C.: IMF, 1970), p. 388.

APPENDIX TABLE 18

Breakdown of Recorded Foreign Trade with Selected Countries, 1964, 1967, and 1969

Country	EXPORTS						IMPORTS					
	1964		1967		1969		1964		1967		1969	
	Amount (million CFAF)	Per Cent	Amount (million CFAF)	Per Cent	Amount (million CFAF)	Per Cent	Amount (million CFAF)	Per Cent	Amount (million CFAF)	Per Cent	Amount (million CFAF)	Per Cent
France	2,310	20	3,480	19	3,935	19.7	2,100	54	4,140	49	4,031	39
EEC (excluding France)	5,075	45	7,850	43	8,466	42.0	495	13	1,020	12	1,459	14
Federal Republic, Germany	2,665		2,970		2,829		450		360		892?	
Belgium-Luxembourg	350		2,150		2,424		20		180		369	
Italy	1,700		2,560		2,654		5		290		109	
Netherlands	360		170		559		20		190		88	
Other Europe	3,100	27	4,380	24	5,545	28.0	150	4	330	4	1,231	12
U.K.	2,980		3,550		4,720		70		190		1,002	
Africa	335	3	480	3	1,248	6.0	35	1	195	2	364	4
UMOA countries	n.a.		6		470		n.a.		73		95	
The Americas	350	3	140	1	70	0.3	890	23	1,565	19	1,747	17
U.S.A.	338		110		34		720		1,200		1,430	
Other countries	150	2	1,900	10	756	4.0	210	5	1,160	14	1,538	14
Japan	120		470		495		--		--		--	
China, Mainland	--		--		--		5		600		768	
Total	11,320	100	18,230	100	20,020	100.0	3,880	100	8,410	100	10,370	100

Source: RIM, BCEAO, "Notes d'Information Statistique: Indicateurs Economiques Mauritaniens," Bulletin Mensuel Statistique, No. 169 (1970).

Foreign Aid and Loans: Government Budgetary and Nonbudgetary Expenditures and Financing, 1960-69
(Million CFAF)

Item	1960	1961	1962	1963	1964	1965	1966	1967	1968	1969*	Average 1960-64	Average 1965-68
EXPENDITURES												
Current Expenditures												
Current budget	3,038	3,412	4,335	4,287	4,117	4,154	4,390	4,916	5,187	6,220	3,838	4,662
Technical assistance (net of local contribution)	350	424	476	545	539	530	579	630	611	570	467	587
Unpaid bills	1	5	7	20	10	17	61	83	130	166	8	73
Total	3,389	3,841	4,818	4,852	4,666	4,701	5,030	5,629	5,928	6,956	4,313	5,322
Current Revenues												
Current budget	1,041	2,341	3,282	3,413	3,766	4,573	4,746	5,191	5,701	5,829	2,769	5,053
Reserve Fund	-	-	-	-	-	-	-	2	50	72	-	13
Equipment Budget	-	120	-	-	-	-	-	-	-	-	24	-
Total	1,041	2,461	3,282	3,413	3,766	4,573	4,746	5,193	5,751	5,901	2,793	5,066
Deficit of current operations	2,348	1,380	1,536	1,439	900	128	284	436	177	1,055	1,520	256
Equipment Expenditures												
Current and equipment budgets	304	442	709	565	448	295	772	689	538	663	493	574
Nonbudgeted foreign aid projects	1,030	1,100	1,505	2,511	1,561	1,415	1,196	2,215	2,796	2,895	1,542	1,905
Investments financed with suppliers' credits	-	-	-	-	-	-	-	65	35	1,086	-	25
Total	1,334	1,542	2,214	3,076	2,009	1,710	1,968	2,969	3,369	4,644	2,035	2,504
Over-all deficit	3,682	2,922	3,750	4,515	2,909	1,838	2,252	3,405	3,546	5,699	3,555	2,760
FINANCING OF OVER-ALL DEFICIT												
Foreign Grant Aid												
French budget subsidies	1,803	1,821	2,254	901	428	291	465	632	177	54	1,441	391
Technical assistance	350	424	476	545	539	530	579	630	611	570	467	588
Nonbudgeted foreign grant aid	930	250	1,369	1,127	1,433	1,367	911	1,651	1,764	1,451	1,022	1,423
Total	3,083	2,495	4,099	2,573	2,400	2,188	1,955	2,913	2,552	2,075	2,930	2,402
Foreign loans at concessionary terms	100	850	136	1,384	128	48	285	564	1,032	1,444	520	482
Short-term Indebtedness												
Suppliers' credits	-	-	-	-	-	-	-	65	35	1,086	-	25
Unpaid bills	1	5	7	20	10	17	61	83	130	166	8	73
Total	1	5	7	20	10	17	61	148	165	1,252	8	98
Changes of treasury reserves (-= increase)	498	-428	-492	538	371	-415	-49	-220	-203	928	97	-222
Total financing items	3,682	2,922	3,750	4,515	2,909	1,838	2,252	3,405	3,546	5,699	3,555	2,760

*Estimates.

Source: RIM, Ministry of Finance, "Comptes Définitifs."

APPENDIX TABLE 20

Net Loan Disbursements of the Caisse Centrale, 1962-69
(Million CFAF)

Recipient	1962	1963	1964	1965	1966	1967	1968	1969
Central government	8	762	774	-123	-2	-127	320	274
Local authorities	1	-1	-1	-1	--	-1	-2	-2
BMD & semi-public enterprises	38	706	-1,097	52	-45	-59	-67	21
Private enterprises	1,400	3,850	--	-100	-113	-278	-314	-513
Total	1,447	5,317	-324	-172	-160	-465	-63	-220

Source: Caisse Centrale de Coopération Economique.

154

APPENDIX TABLE 21

Caisse Centrale Financing in Mauritania, 1961-67
(Million CFA)

| End of Period | Public Sector | | Private Sector | Grand Total |
	Total	BMD Portion		
December 31, 1961	1,692	-	2,500	4,192
December 31, 1962	1,828	20	3,900	5,728
December 31, 1963	3,212	159	7,750	10,962
December 31, 1964	2,889	287	7,750	10,639
December 31, 1965	2,814	333	7,650	10,464
December 31, 1966	2,755	292	7,541	10,296
September 30, 1967	2,605	266	7,485	10,090

Source: Conjoncture Ouest Africaine, No. 137 (February, 1967) and No. 149 (March, 1968).

Estimated Central Government,
Foreign Debt and Service Payments, 1969
(Thousand CFAF)

Lender	Date	Interest Rate	Original Amount	Outstanding as of December 31, 1969	1969 Amortization	1969 Interest	1969 Total
Caisse Centrale de Coopéra-tion Economique	1957	2.5	60,000	30,701	3,006	824	3,830
	1960	2.2	9,907	4,085	614	100	714
	1962	1.0	{563,537	520,501	9,145	5,274	14,419
			{15,000	--	--	--	--
	1963	2.5	770,000	462,200	51,300	12,388	63,688
	1964	4.5	892,333	505,380	71,874	25,176	97,050
	1966	3.5	120,000	96,000	24,000	4,263	28,263
	1967	3.5	17,000	11,802	--	413	413
	1968	6.0	825,000	825,000	--	45,118	45,118
	1968	3.5	50,000	50,000	--	1,777	1,777
French Treasury	--	3.0	20,750	11,903	--	--	--
	--	3.5-6.5	16,412	2,919	293	163	456
FAC	1966	3.0	140,000	140,000	--	4,258	4,258
	1966	1.0	250,000	250,000	--	2,500	2,500
	1968	1.0	31,000	29,230	--	310	310
	1968	3.0	80,000	29,983	--	912	912
IDA	1969	0.5	75,000	46,067	--	--	--
	1964	0.75	1,653,915	948,524	--	--	--
Total				3,964,295	160,232	103,476	263,708

Source: Surveys of African Economies, Vol. III: Mauritania (Washington, D. C.: IMF, 1970), p. 398.

APPENDIX TABLE 23
Road Transport, 1959-69

Item	1959	1964	1967	1969
Road Network (in km.)[a]				
Paved roads	n.a.	n.a.	96	280
Laterite roads	n.a.	980	1,105	1,181
Total all-weather roads	n.a.	980	1,201	1,461
Other national roads	n.a.	2,205	2,065	2,065
Tracks	n.a.	2,815	2,860	2,860
Number of Licensed Motor Vehicles (as of December 31)				
Automobiles	225	1,390	2,996	4,161
Buses	25	38	39	54
Trucks & vans	1,545	2,377	3,858	4,962
Special vehicles	91	484	201	242
Road tractors	22	121	127	157
Total	1,908	4,410	7,221	9,576
Consumption of Some Petroleum Products (in thousand m.^{3})				
Gasoline	3.5	9.3	12.4	12.9
Gas-oil[b]	10.8	32.5	38.3	43.3

[a] Excluding urban streets.
[b] Of which it was estimated that some 20 per cent is used for road-transport purposes.

Source: RIM, Bulletin Statistique et Economique.

APPENDIX

B

COMMUNITY DEVELOPMENT:
THE CHANTIERS
DE DÉVELOPPEMENT

The Chantiers de Développement came into existence through a 1963 law. They are administered by the Ministry of Labor and Health. Their basic purpose was to foster local investments in such works as rural dams, wells, schools, dispensaries, roads, and housing in order to relieve rural unemployment, particularly that resulting from the release of large numbers of workers engaged in the construction phase of the large industrial complexes in the north. Further, they were intended to eliminate seasonal underemployment in the rural and semiurban areas.

Projects for community development under the program are supposed to emanate from the Communes and to be approved by the Commune Councils as a means of stimulating local initiative and leadership. The criteria for approval are as follows:

1. The project must respond to some local need.
2. The project must be based on a simple technology requiring a minimum of specialized personnel.
3. The project must be studied and approved by the technical services of the Ministry.

Workers are generally paid daily with consumption goods. Credits are allocated for equipment and transportation. Financing is obtained from the Communes, the state budget, and U.S. aid, the latter in the form of foodstuffs and matériel. The government-appointed Chief of the Subdivision, who is also Chairman or President of Pilot Communes, is the operational head of each project. Until 1966, the Chantiers had insufficient finances and personnel. Since then, the administration and execution of projects has been improved with the addition of French personnel fulfilling their military obligations, as well as about twelve U.S. Peace Corps members.*

In 1964, the Chantiers started with 137 projects, requiring

---

*The United States' part of the program was suspended when Mauritania broke diplomatic relations during the 1967 Middle East crisis.

some 200,000 days of work. The work accomplished had an estimated value of CFAF 90 million and required 1,800 tons of food distributed under U.S. PL 480. No work was undertaken in 1965. In 1966, a further 153 projects were prepared. In total, from 1963 through 1967, the state budget contributed CFAF 89 million; and the U.S. Agency for International Development (AID) gave about 2,500 tons of food, worth some CFAF 30 million, and CFAF 8-10 million in vehicles and diverse equipment. The Communes also budgeted some funds. Between 300,000 and 350,000 days of work were provided by local workers, with a value of about CFAF 75 million.

In conclusion, 314 projects were carried out through 1967, a large number of which were poorly executed. Nevertheless, considerable community interest was awakened in the programs. With improved organization and staffing, the program of the Chantiers could accomplish a good deal in the way of planned local public works under the forthcoming development program, while giving the local communities a real sense of participation and accomplishment. A program of this type assumes particular importance in Mauritania, which lacks a large and well-trained central administrative apparatus, but which must concentrate on rural programs of development in order to raise the standard of living of the bulk of the people.

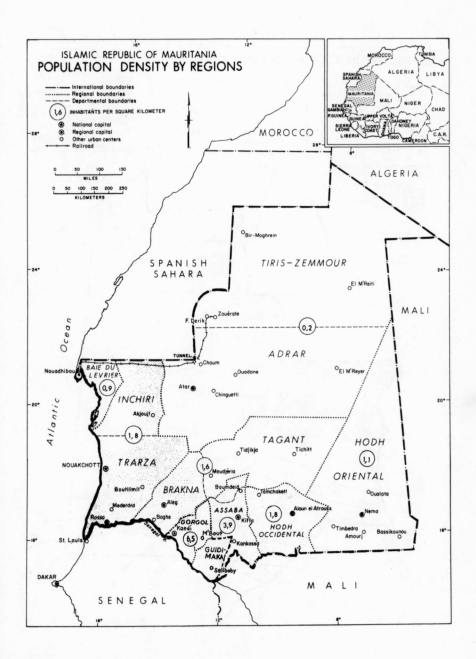

ISLAMIC REPUBLIC OF MAURITANIA
POPULATION DENSITY BY REGIONS

International boundaries
Regional boundaries
Departmental boundaries

1,6 INHABITANTS PER SQUARE KILOMETER
⊛ National capital
◉ Regional capital
○ Other urban centers
┼┼┼ Railroad

0   50   100   150
MILES

0 50 100 150 200 250
KILOMETERS

MOROCCO

ALGERIA

SPANISH
SAHARA

TIRIS – ZEMMOUR

MALI

Bir-Moghrein

El M'Reiti

Zouérate
F. Derik
TUNNEL
Choum

ADRAR

0,2

Ouadane

El M'Reyer

Nouadhibou

BAIE DU
LEVRIER

0,9

INCHIRI

Atar

Chinguetti

Akjoujt

1,8

TRARZA

NOUAKCHOTT

TAGANT

Tidjikja   Tichitt

Moudjéria

1,6

HODH

1,1

ORIENTAL

Boutilimit

BRAKNA

Aleg

Boghe

Baumdeid

ASSABA

Tamchakett

Ouatata

1,8

Aioun el Atrouss

Nema

Mederdra

Rosso

GORGOL

Kaedi

M'Bout

6,5

3,9

Kiffa

HODH
OCCIDENTAL

Timbedra
Amourj

Bassikounou

St. Louis

GUIDI-
MAKA

Kankossa

Selibaby

DAKAR

SENEGAL

M A L I

Ocean

Atlantic

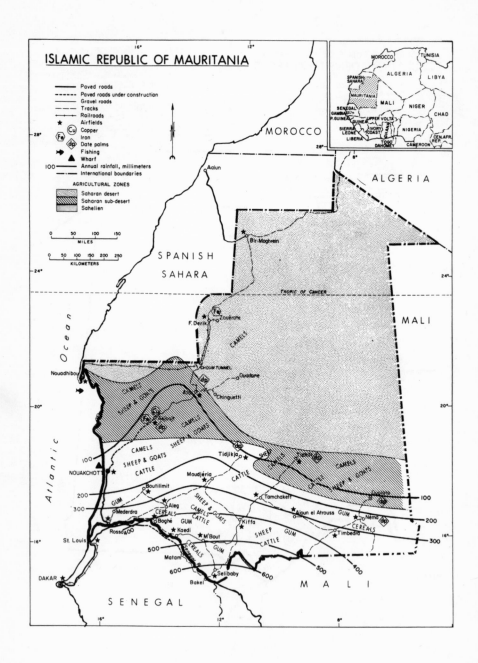

ISLAMIC REPUBLIC OF MAURITANIA

Paved roads
Paved roads under construction
Gravel roads
Tracks
Railroads
★ Airfields
Cu Copper
Fe Iron
dp Date palms
Fishing
▲ Wharf
100 Annual rainfall, millimeters
International boundaries
AGRICULTURAL ZONES
Saharan desert
Saharan sub-desert
Sahelien

MILES
0   50   100   150

KILOMETERS
0   50   100   150   200   250

MOROCCO

ALGERIA

SPANISH
SAHARA

MALI

Aalun

Bir-Moghrein

TROPIC OF CANCER

F. Derik   Zouérate

Nouadhibou

CHOUM TUNNEL   Ouadane

Chinguetti

Atar

Fort Gouraud

Tidjikja

NOUAKCHOTT

Moudjéria

Tichitt

Boutilimit

CAMELS

SHEEP & GOATS

CATTLE

Tamchakett

Oualata

Aleg

Mederdra

Boghé

Kiffa

Aioun el Atrouss   Néma

Rosso

Kaedi   M'Bout

CEREALS

St. Louis

Matam

Timbedra

DAKAR

Selibaby

Bakel

SENEGAL

MALI

Ocean

Atlantic

166

SELECTED BIBLIOGRAPHY

BOOKS AND ARTICLES

Boutiller, J. L. , Coutrelle, P. , Caussé, J. Laurent, C. ,
N'Doye, Th. La Moyenne Vallée du Sénégal. Paris:
Ministère de la Coopération, 1962.

Daumas, J. C. Bilan des Etudes Economiques dans la Vallée
du Sénégal. Bulletin No. 128 (June, 1961).

Désiré Vuillemin, Geneviève. Contribution à l'Histoire de la
Mauritanie, 1900-1934. Dakar: Edition Clairafrique,
1962.

Dubois, Jean Paul. La Basse Vallée du Gorgol: Etude de
Géographie Régionale. Paris: Mission d'aménagement
du Fleuve Sénégal, Bulletin No. 133 (February, 1962).

Eagleton, William, L. "The Islamic Republic of Mauritania, "
Middle East Journal. Winter, 1965, pp. 45-53.

Garnier, Christine. Désert Fertile Un Nouvel Etat: La
Mauritanie. Paris: Librairie Hachette, 1960.

Lacoume, François. Eléments pour une Stratégie du Développement de la Mauritanie: Influence du Renversement du
Circuit Economique (thesis presented for the doctor's
degree 3rd cycle, Faculté des Lettres et des Sciences
Humaines de l'Université de Paris), September, 1968.

Marc, Clément H. "One Partyism in Mauritania, " Journal
of Modern African Studies, 3 (1965). Institute of International Studies, Reprint No. 245.

Pujos, Jérome. Croissance Economique et Impulsion
Extérieure: Etude sur l'Economie Mauritanienne. (Etudes
Economiques Internationales). Paris: Presses Universi-
taires de France, 1964.

OFFICIAL PUBLICATIONS AND REPORTS

Bureau pour le Développement de la Production Agricole
(B. D. P. A.), Operation de Modernisation Rurale dans la
Vallée du Fleuve: Rapport Annuel, 1963. Paris: R. I. M.,
1964.

_____. Possibilités de développement des cultures
vivrières dans la zone fluviale du Sud-Est mauritanien
(report by Gorse, Jean, Lanien, Christian). Paris:
B. D. P. A. , 1967.

_____. Proposition pour l'utilisation d'un aménagement
hydro-agricole de la Plaine de Boghe. Paris: R. I. M.,
Ministère de l'Economie Rurale, 1966.

Bulletin Statistique et Economique 1964. Nouakchott: R. I. M.,
Service de la Statistique.

Bulletin Statistique et Economique, Situation de l'Emploi
Salarié en 1965. Nouakchott: R. I. M., Direction Générale
du Travail, Service de la Statistique, 1966.

Caisse Nationale de Sécurité Sociale. Rapport d'Activité,
Année 1966. Nouakchott: R. I. M.

Comité Inter-Etats pour l'Aménagement du Bassin du Fleuve
Sénégal. Proposition concernant la Coopération pour le
Développement Economique (Enquête Menée du 1er juin
au 15 septembre 1966), Vol. I, pp. 1-421; Vol. II, pp.
422-6701.

Direction du Plan, R. I. M. Plan Quadriennal 1963-1966, Bilan
de trois années d'exécution. Nouakchott: Service de la
Statistique, 1967.

Direction du Plan, R. I. M. Plan Quadriennal 1963-1967,
Bilan d'exécution. Nouakchott: Ministère des Affaires
étrangères et du Plan (R. I. M.), December, 1967.

Direction des Douanes, Ministère des Finances, R. I. M.
Douanes Mauritaniennes Organisation Règlementation,
R. I. M.: March, 1968 (unpublished).

Lacrouts, M. Tyc, and Clement, P. Exploitation du Bétail
Mauritanien: Projet d'expédition de viandes foraine à
partir de Kaédi. Paris: Ministère pour l'Aide et la
Coopération de la Republique Française, October, 1961-
January, 1962.

Moktar Ould Daddah. "Allocation à l'occasion de l'inauguration
des installations Miferma à Zourate," June 15, 1963
(unpublished).

_____. "Rapport sur l'Etat de la Nation présenté à
l'Assemblée Nationale," November 28, 1969 (unpublished).

Moktar Ould Haiba. Exposé Introductif du Ministre de la
Planification et du Développement Rural à l'occasion du
Séminaire des Gouverneurs, Secrétaires Fédéraux et
Présidents des Commissions Régionales, Nouakchott:
January 27-30, 1969 (unpublished).

IIIe Congrès Ordinaire du Parti du Peuple Mauritanien.
Brochure éditée par les services de la Permanence du
Parti (Containing speech by Moktar Ould Daddah and
General Resolutions of the 3rd regular Congress, 23,
24, 25, 26, 27 January, 1968). Nouakchott, 1968.

Ministère de la Planification et du Développement Rural,
Direction de la Statistique et des Etudes Economiques,
R. I. M. Comptes Economiques de la République Islamique
de Mauritanie. Nouakchott, 1968.

Ministère de la Planification et du Développement Rural,
R. I. M. Deuxième Plan de Développement Economique
et Social 1970-1973. Nouakchott, 1970.

_____. Annuaire statistique 1968. Nouakchott: Direction
de la Statistique, R. I. M. , 1969.

_____. Mise en valeur du Bassin du Gorgol (Requête
du Programme des Nations Unies pour le Développement),
Vol. I, pp. 1-44; Vol. II, pp. 1-63 (Nouakchott: Juin,
1968).

République Islamique de Mauritanie (R. I. M.). Budget de
l'Etat pour l'année 1969 (Nouakchott). Vol. pp. 1-160;
Vol. II, pp. 148-327.

_____. La Mauritanie, Etat minier. Ministère des Finances, du Travail et des Affaires Economiques, Service des Mines et de la Géologie, May 29, 1964.

_____. Plan Quadriennal de Développement Economique et Social, 1963-66. Paris: R.I.M., 1964.

Secrétariat du Comité Monétaire de la Zone Franc. La Zone Franc en 1965. Paris: Imprimerie Nationale, 1966.

Société d'Etudes pour le Développement Economique et Social (S.E.D.E.S.). Enquête Démographique 1964-1965. Paris: R.I.M., October, 1966.

_____. L'Enfance et la Jeunesse dans le Développement de la Mauritanie. Paris: R.I.M., 1967.

_____. Les échanges Commerciaux en Mauritanie. Paris: R.I.M., November, 1968. Vol. I, pp. 1-204; Vol. II, pp. 1-257.

_____. Proposition pour l'Amélioration de l'Infrastructure des Transports en Mauritanie. Paris: Ministère de la Coopération, April, 1963.

Traités et Accords de Coopération France-Mauritanie. Journal Officiel de la République Française. Paris: Imprimerie des Journaux Officiels (No. 0223), February, 1962.

Richard M. Westebbe, Chief of the Economics of Urbanization Division of the IBRD, has had considerable experience in
foreign aid and international development. He was Nether-
lands Desk Officer in the Marshall Plan, economist working
on U. K. -Sterling area matters in the Federal Reserve Board,
and, for six years, Executive Director of the Greek Government's Foreign Trade Administration.

He joined the IBRD in 1966 and successively headed its
technical assistance mission to Mauritania and its economic
mission to Morocco. He was appointed to his present post in
late 1968 in order to develop a basis for the IBRD's policies
and programs in the new field of urbanization. He has traveled
extensively while with the IBRD.

Mr. Westebbe did his undergraduate work at Georgetown
School of Foreign Service and some graduate work at its
Graduate School. He did most of his postgraduate work in
economics at Harvard University's Graduate School of Arts
and Sciences and held a Littauer Fellowship while at Harvard
and a Fulbright Scholarship in Holland. He has taught economics at Georgetown and at the Higher Economics and Commercial School of Athens. He was a consultant to the Center
for Planning and Economic Research while in Greece. He
has co-authored several books and has written numerous
articles during the course of his career.